# MY COUNTRY

## GEORGE CANYON

Published by Simon & Schuster

New York   London   Toronto   Sydney   New Delhi

SIMON &
SCHUSTER
CANADA

Simon & Schuster Canada
A Division of Simon & Schuster, Inc.
166 King Street East, Suite 300
Toronto, Ontario M5A 1J3

This Simon & Schuster Canada edition November 2022

SIMON & SCHUSTER CANADA and colophon are trademarks of
Simon & Schuster, Inc.

For information about special discounts for bulk purchases, please contact Simon &
Schuster Special Sales at 1-800-268-3216 or CustomerService@simonandschuster.ca.

Manufactured in the United States of America

1   3   5   7   9   10   8   6   4   2

Library and Archives Canada Cataloguing in Publication
Title: My country / George Canyon
Names: Canyon, George, author.
Identifiers: Canadiana (print) 2022026726X | Canadiana (ebook) 20220267383 | ISBN
9781982196882 (softcover) | ISBN 9781982196899 (ebook)
Subjects: LCSH: Canyon, George. | LCSH: Singers—Canada—Biography. | LCSH:
Country musicians—Canada—Biography. | LCGFT: Autobiographies.
Classification: LCC ML420.C135 A3 2022 | DDC 782.421642092—dc23

ISBN 978-1-9821-9688-2
ISBN 978-1-9821-9689-9 (ebook)

To my wife, Jennifer: my best friend, the love of my life, and my rock. I would be completely lost without you.

To my children, for understanding why Dad wasn't there so many times, and for supporting and loving me anyway.

To my mom and dad, who laid the foundations of my faith, and the love of my country.

And last but not least, to all of my family, my friends, and my fans: thank you for being a part of this journey called life, and for your support through all the years.

# CONTENTS

# MY COUNTRY

# PROLOGUE

I t was May 1, 2004, and I was standing underneath the blinding lights of the hallowed Grand Ole Opry theatre in front of a screaming, sold-out crowd—not to mention millions of viewers on TV—waiting to hear the sentence that would change my life.

It was the final night of *Nashville Star*, a reality show for country musicians in its second season. I'd spent the last five months of my life here, in the heart of the country music industry, and now my mind flashed back to all the steps along the way that had brought me to this moment: not just the nerve-racking auditions in Calgary and Philadelphia, but also the decade-plus I'd spent on the road touring dive bars and music joints across Canada. Over the years, I had seen just about every inch of this great country of ours as I tried to scrape together a music career after I abandoned a promising future in medicine—a decision that gave my loving parents back home in Nova Scotia no shortage of heartache and worry.

Somehow, I'd made it onto *Nashville Star* as its only Canadian contestant, then survived all eight eliminations along the way. That's how I ended up here, waiting to see which name the announcer was going to call out as the winner: Brad Cotter, Matt Lindahl, or me. One of us was going to get a record deal with Sony, and from there the path to stardom wasn't difficult to imagine. The other two? Well, let's just say the future was a lot hazier.

Of course, in TV, they know to milk a moment like that for all it's worth. So just as it seemed they were finally about to announce the winner, the cameras cut to one last commercial break.

I let out a breath. I'd stood before a lot of crowds by that point in my career, but I never felt so excited—or so queasy—in front of an audience as I did that evening in Nashville. The whole show had been a surreal experience for me. As a kid growing up in little Pictou County, Nova Scotia, my dreams didn't involve playing music at all. But a surprise trip to the hospital when I was fourteen changed my life's trajectory, and suddenly I had to reckon with the fact that nothing was going to go the way I'd imagined it would.

Back then, I could never have dreamed that one day I'd find myself here, standing on one of the most famous stages in the world. Or that I'd have already worked out a deal with one of country music's best managers, who had big plans of his own for my future. Or that I'd have a beautiful wife and two amazing kids to cheer me on from back home in Canada.

As the cameras turned back on, I found myself starting to giggle. Sure, I had no idea what was about to happen, or where my future might lead me. But I'd already dealt with so much uncertainty in my life, and I'd always tried to face it with a smile and a sense of humour. Why should a moment like this be any different?

I gave Brad and Matt one last nod of solidarity, then turned to the judges and waited for their verdict. No matter what was about to happen, I was ready for it.

## Chapter One

# PICTOU COUNTY

S omeone asked me how old I was when I first started playing music. I have vivid memories of sitting around the kitchen table as a little kid, listening to my mother sing while my grandpa played the guitar. I knew "Danny Boy" from hearing it on records and on the radio, but it was incredible to see it being played right in front of me. It triggered something inside me, and soon enough I convinced my parents to give me an old acoustic guitar. They taught me three chords, and I was off to the races. Every morning I sat on our old green couch and practiced my guitar until the second I had to run down and catch the bus to school. Then, when I got back home again, I'd grab a snack and then get right back to it. I took to that guitar like a fish takes to water.

But music wasn't my first love. When I was five years old—I remember it like it was yesterday—I wanted nothing more than to be an astronaut.

It's kind of strange. A lot of people wonder if it's something

I made up, or a faulty memory or something, given the different paths life would eventually take me down. But it's the truth. As far back as I can remember, I wanted to ride an Apollo rocket all the way to the moon.

I'm not sure where the idea came from. It's not like my family had any experience with zero gravity. My dad was the chief technologist at the local hospital, and my mom worked at a lawyer's office. They had good jobs and were saving up to build a house, but for the first few years of my life, my parents, my two younger sisters, Cynthia and Mylissa, and I lived in a single-wide trailer in the middle of rural Nova Scotia. I remember sitting in that trailer, watching replays of the 1969 lunar landing on our old black-and-white TV, and dreaming about a life in the stars. Seeing those images of the earth from outer space really put things in perspective and made me realize there was way more to the universe than just us humans.

I'm not sure what everyone else thought about this dream of mine, but eventually Dad made a suggestion that got my mind racing in a slightly more realistic direction. He said, "You know, before you become an astronaut, first you have to be in the air force. You have to be a pilot and learn how to fly a plane here on earth."

That made sense to me—so from then on, airplanes became my new obsession. I stared at them whenever they flew past overhead, I stopped channel surfing anytime I saw them on TV, and I read everything I could find about them (or at least everything I could understand at that young age).

So at five years old, I had my whole life figured out. I was going to become a pilot in the air force, then eventually upgrade to being an astronaut, and it was all going to work out great. My entire life was planned out. Easy!

I've always heard it said that if you want to make the Lord laugh, tell Him your plans. Well, I did. And then so did He.

To understand the many paths that life has led me down over the years, you first have to understand the place my family and I come from. I was born in 1970, in a little community on the north shore of Nova Scotia called Pictou County, right outside a town called Westville. There were a whole bunch of little towns in the area, and all of them served a purpose. Westville was a coal town. Pictou was where the harbour was, which opened up into Northumberland Strait and on to the Atlantic Ocean, so it was responsible for making ships. Trenton made trains at their steelworks. Stellarton was responsible for getting the coal onto the ships and trains, and Thorburn was a support community. In order to survive and grow, these towns all had to work together—along with the Mi'kmaq, obviously, who have lived in that area for a long time before we ever got there. Pictou is also famous for being the place where the ship *Hector* landed in 1773, bearing a boatload of Canada's first immigrants from Scotland—including some members of my own family. Our roots in this country date all the way back to the eighteenth century, and we've maintained a strong connection to the area ever since.

Growing up in Pictou County, nothing was more important than family. With so many of my relatives living in the county, everything we did was a family affair with my grandparents, uncles, aunts, and cousins all involved. My sister Cynthia always wanted to tag along with whatever I was doing, no matter whether it was riding bikes or playing bows and arrows, and like any good big brother I indulged her as much as I could. Mylissa was several years younger, so our paths didn't cross as often, but we still spent plenty of time skiing and tobogganing together.

On a typical Sunday, we'd all go to church first thing in the morning, which was my introduction to music. I loved singing, and would belt out the hymns as loudly as I could, even though I could barely see over the top of the pew in front of me. Luckily, it was a lively congregation, and everybody else sang along with me—especially Mom, a tall and strong-willed woman who stood at the front as a member of the choir. On top of being a talented musician who performed all over the county, she was also a lector, and each week would get up and read Scripture in front of everyone. But for me, it was all about the music.

After church, all of us cousins would go down to visit my grandparents on my dad's side, who lived in one of the coal mining houses built for families of the workers. These tended to be real small. Just one floor, two rooms (if you were lucky), paper insulation in the walls, and a big stove in the centre—heated by coal, naturally. Each fall, we would go collect seaweed and line the bottom of the entire house with it to create more insulation, so that the cold air couldn't get in underneath the floor. It smelled awful. But I've got to admit, I miss that smell now.

My grandmother was a little sweetheart of a lady, and while I referred to her as Nanny, all of the adults called her Honey. It took me years to realize that wasn't her real name. As a kid, you don't even think to ask questions like that. I just thought,

*Oh yeah, it's George and Honey.* (Her real name, I found out much later, was Alvina.) And, like a lot of men of that era, my grandfather, who I called Papa, was a miner. He used to tell me stories about working in the coal mine, like the canaries they would carry down in cages with them. If the canary ever fell over and passed out, that meant the miners had hit a pocket of methane gas, which was incredibly dangerous, because if there was any kind of spark, then the gas would explode and the mine would cave in. He knew a lot of people who'd died that way. Papa always told me he was lucky that he only ended up getting miner's lung. I don't know how lucky he really was because he could barely breathe. All that dust worked its way into his lungs, and it just didn't come back out. He was on asthma medication and could barely leave the house—until it came to hunting season, of course, at which point he'd be right out there with all my uncles.

When we visited them after church, Papa would be sitting there whittling a piece of wood with a jackknife, and Nanny would be making biscuits, or pie, or something else equally delicious in the kitchen. You name it, she knew how to bake it. One time I asked Nanny if I could help with her baking, and she said, "Sure, you can sift the flour." It's funny how you associate certain memories and objects with people. Nowadays, I don't sift flour anymore, and neither does my wife. But we were recently making bannock at a campsite and her cousin brought out a flour sifter—and it was the exact same one my nanny had. One glance, and it felt like I was right back in that kitchen with her again.

We spent hours at their little place, enjoying quality time as a family. But it could be dangerous having so many people in such a small space. Just ask my uncle Tommy. He's one of my dad's younger brothers, and he was notorious for putting his feet inside the stove to keep them warm in the harsh Nova Scotia winters. One time, he fell asleep in his chair and lit his socks on fire. As kids, us cousins couldn't stop giggling, even though we were jammed in right next to him. In fact, the whole family was just about crying laughing—except for Tommy, who was doing this odd-looking jig, trying to keep his socks from going up in flames.

In the summers, our family would go camping at a nearby place called Black Brook Lake. We would catch trout and Nanny would cook them up. But she could catch 'em, too. I remember watching her standing at the side of the lake, throwing out the cast with a bobber and worm. Then she'd immediately sit back down and start smoking these cigarettes that she rolled herself by hand. All of us kids were fascinated by this and used to sit at the kitchen table trying to figure out how she did it. Later on, she developed rheumatoid arthritis— but she never lost her ability to roll her cigarettes. Anyway, despite having a (shall we say) unusual approach to fishing, Nanny still managed to catch trout like nobody's business. Sometimes even she wouldn't notice. We'd have to yell, "Honey, you got another one!" And Papa would laugh and laugh at her good luck.

In general, Papa didn't say much. He was a pretty quiet man. But he was—and I say this with love—the greatest bullshitter in the world. My papa could tell you a story and you would believe every word of it. He did just that to us kids, all the time. When I was around six or seven, I already loved being in the woods, even though I wasn't good at hunting or fishing. So one day Papa said, "Little Fred"—which is what they called me, because I was Frederick George, Jr., named after both my dad and my papa—"come over here and sit on my knee. I'm going to tell you how to catch a rabbit." He proceeded to tell me this complicated plan that involved a sapling, a rock, a rope, a stick, and a carrot. They were all supposed to be connected and tied together, so that when a rabbit came along and ate the carrot, he ended up getting crushed by the falling rock. I didn't quite follow the ins and outs of the plan, but I was sure Papa had just let me in on an amazing secret. *I'm going to be the greatest hunter ever!* Over the next week I spent hours in the woods, trying to build this rabbit trap. But when it inevitably didn't work, I never blamed Papa. I knew it must've been my fault, that somehow I couldn't remember how to do it exactly the way he'd told me. It just was another way Papa was an impressive man in my mind, and, in a way, I would spend the rest of my life trying to live up to his example.

As a kid, I didn't realize how lucky I was to always be surrounded by family. It was such a basic part of my life that I didn't understand or appreciate how important it was. But families tend to be large in Nova Scotia. (What can I say? Cold winters.) So if I wasn't visiting with Nanny and Papa, then chances are I was with my grandparents on my mom's side. I was blessed in this respect because my nanny divorced her first husband and got remarried before I was born. So where most people have four grandparents, at most, I was fortunate enough to grow up with five.

My mom's dad, to me, was a giant. His name was Bill Westerman, and when I was young I thought he was nine feet tall.

Looking back on it, he was probably more like 6'4" or 6'5". But still: a big fella, no doubt about it, with hands the size of footballs and a kind, gentle demeanour. We would go fishing together, and as I grew up I slowly learned more about his time serving in World War II. He didn't really talk about it on his own—but not for the reasons we often hear about now, where soldiers suffer from post-traumatic stress disorder, or PTSD. No, in his case, the army simply refused to send him out to the front.

It took a long time to finally get the story out of him. Back then, stepping up to fight for your country—especially against an enemy as strong and fearsome as the Nazis—was a matter of pride. Everyone wanted to be part of it. There are stories of young men who didn't qualify, whether because of medical reasons or otherwise, who went on to commit suicide. They just couldn't deal with not being a part of the war effort. My grandpa was like that. It was critical to him that he serve his country and fight for freedom. So he joined the army along with all of his brothers and friends, and they got on a ship in Halifax and sailed to England, where the Allied troops were mustered.

When they got there, one of the things my grandpa and the others learned is that the army had certain pieces of equipment that were so large, they could only be used by soldiers who were similarly big and strong. One of these was a bazooka. Well, the army recruiters took one look at my grandpa, who had no problem holding a bazooka—heck, he could probably hold two, one on each shoulder, if he had to—and told him he wasn't going to be leaving England after all. They said, "We're keeping you here to train other soldiers how to fire a bazooka like you do." That's because, in addition to being strong, my grandpa was an amazing shot, and could fire one of those rocket launchers as accurately as another soldier could fire a .22.

It was a compliment to his abilities as a marksman, but the news really hit my grandpa hard. He wanted to go and fight. He wanted to serve. And he didn't feel like his assignment in England was good enough. It affected him for the rest of his life, and later drove him to drink, in order to deal with the guilt he felt. (My papa on my dad's side didn't serve, either, because his work in the mines rendered him unfit for duty. I'm sure that weighed heavily on him, too.)

None of that mattered to me, though. I was just in awe of the fact that he'd served in the war at all, and I used to love getting a peek at his old coin collections and medals. I still have some of his war memorabilia today, and it means the world to me. At those visits back in the day, I soaked up every word my grandpa said—because I wanted to be in the air force, and he was ex-military. I figured he would have words of wisdom for me. While he knew I was interested, for whatever reason, he never tried to influence my decision one way or the other. He never said, "Sure, join the air force. You'll have a blast!" But there was no discouragement, either. It was like he knew the decision was mine alone to make.

In the end, Grandpa was lucky enough to get over his alcoholism, and he did so through a funny method: baking muffins. Whenever we went down to his place for brunch, he would always have these trays of muffins ready for us, hot and fresh out of the oven. What's even funnier is I can't remember him ever eating them himself. He just baked them, and for him that was therapy, in its own way.

By the time I was around ten years old, I learned my cousin Buddy was an actual, real-life air force pilot. Whenever he was around, I would hang off his every word for stories about the military. Buddy had flown fighter jets in Korea, and he had more positive memories about his service than my grandpa did, so he talked about it a lot more. It was so cool to me, to have someone in the family who was doing the exact same thing I wanted to do.

While I waited for my chance to take flight, I passed the time in Pictou County with a bunch of other hobbies and interests. At the top of that list was hockey. I started skating at age four, and picked up my first hockey stick not long after that. I played on a team called, appropriately enough, the Westville Miners, at an arena that was unbelievably cold. Arenas didn't have heaters back then, or at least not small-town ones like mine. Sometimes, the air itself became a hazard. If the humidity got too high, we would head out on the ice for a practice and there would be so much fog you couldn't see the other players. And this was an indoor arena! Suffice to say, our team developed reflexes that were second to none. You had no choice but learn how to move fast and react quickly when other players were jumping out of the fog and scaring the snot out of you. I loved hockey so much that it even crept into my mind as a secondary dream. *Maybe*, I thought to myself as I dodged opposing players emerging from the mists, *maybe one day I'll be good enough to be in the NHL.*

Now, as a kid, I had such a strong relationship with my Lord and saviour, Jesus Christ, that I would just talk to Him wherever I was, like He was my buddy sitting next to me. I'm sure God had to put in earplugs, the amount of time that I wouldn't shut up. I'd ask God to help me catch a fish from the brook, and I'd thank Him when I got a particularly good grade at school. I remember the exact day I asked to make it to the NHL.

"Wouldn't it be so cool, Lord?" I asked.

Again, I wasn't officially praying. I was just talking. But there's another old saying: *Be careful what you wish for*. This was a great example of that. Because you have to remember, God answers prayers in the best way He sees fit. My dad once explained it to me this way: "We're His children, and He wants to make us happy. But He also knows what's best for us."

Looking back on it, I should've been a little more specific. After all, I'd prayed not to *play* in the NHL, but to *be* in the NHL. Years later, I got hired to sing the national anthems for the Calgary Flames—and what's funny is that I am actually on the roster. If you look at an official game sheet, the anthem singer is listed, way down on the very last line. So maybe I did make the NHL after all. At least technically.

One of the main spots I would sit and talk with God was this beautiful little brook—out west we'd call it a creek—a few acres behind my parents' house. A budding amateur fisherman, I would go down there every day in the summer. You had to walk down a dirt road and look for this one particular hole, which I recognized as the perfect fishing spot. There was a little culvert under the road that was made of railway ties, and to this day, whenever I smell creosol, it brings back a flood of memories of sitting at that brook for hours. Anyway, I'd plop down there and chat with the Lord as I changed the worm on my hook every five minutes because I was so impatient. Every now and again, I'd be extra blessed, and actually catch something. This was where I told God all about my dreams of flying to the stars.

The truth was, my dream was even bigger than the rest of my family knew. Really, it was all I thought about. There was a little hill by the trees near our house, and I used to run as fast as I could and then leap off the top, just so I could feel the briefest sensation of flight. But when Mom and Dad asked me, "Why do you want to do this again?" I didn't really have an answer for them. I just knew that, thanks to my relationship with the Lord, I was meant to fly. It felt like a built-in dream that came in two parts—first the air force, then space—and I knew that I needed to fulfil it, no matter what. Hadn't I told the Lord?

## Chapter Two

# LIFTOFF AND CRASH

From the moment I turned eleven years old, I was focused on one thing: turning twelve. Usually, my birthday wasn't that big of a deal to me. I was mostly just happy to have an excuse to open a few gifts and eat a big slice of cake. (This remains one of my weaknesses to this day. When there's nothing else in the house for dessert, I'll often ask my wife, Jen, to drop by a Sobeys and pick up one of their cheap vanilla cakes for us to split. It's not anyone's birthday or anything. I just like cake.)

But my twelfth birthday was different. That was the age that I was officially allowed to enlist in air cadets. It was the first step towards my dream of being in the military—and, hopefully, one day blasting off into outer space.

One of the things that inspired me about the military was all the time I'd spent as a kid watching Dad shoot. He was, and remains, the best marksman I ever saw. Dad wasn't tall—maybe 5'9" or 5'10"—but he was a kind and principled man, with a beautiful moustache, who was driven in everything he did. He was also a man of his word, and his handshake meant everything. When it came to firearms, Dad not only built his own rifles, but helped other people get theirs ready and sighted for hunting season. He also shot competitively throughout the '70s, winning awards and even joining the Canadian national team. Dad's weapon of choice was a big-bore rifle, which was a .308 calibre, and open sights, so no scope to help you aim. At competitions they would have to shoot at targets at various distances, and as a kid I would tag along to cheer my dad on.

I remember at one particular competition, Dad was getting ready to shoot open sights at 1,000 yards. The targets were large, but that didn't matter. A thousand yards is a thousand yards. To even come close to hitting a target at that distance, Dad had to be incredibly precise, taking into account things like windage and repositioning himself accordingly. It was a learned skill. Most of it was basically just math, but applied in a far cooler way than any of my teachers at school were showing me.

Anyway, the problem was my sister Cynthia and I got chicken pox right in the middle of the shoot. It was not a pleasant experience. We were so itchy we could hardly move, and because we were still contagious, we had to wait in the camper while Dad went out and finished shooting. Now, at these events, you have to shoot standing, kneeling, and lying down. In this case, Dad ended up lying down directly on top of an anthill—and not just any anthill, but a red anthill. He was up there for probably twenty or thirty minutes, and the entire time he was getting eaten alive by these hungry, angry ants. Somehow, though, Dad managed to see the funny side of it all. When he finally came back to the trailer to see us, he pointed at all these welts on his stomach and chest and told us that he had chicken pox, too.

Our mantel at home was full of Dad's trophies, medals, and old photographs from all of the competitions he'd attended over the years. To be clear, he wasn't a proud guy, and showing off his achievements like this wasn't his idea. It was Mom's, and he reluctantly went along with it. I used to study all these mementos, and one photograph in particular still sticks in my mind. It was of Dad, along with the rest of the Atlantic team. At the time, whoever won the shoot would sit in a chair, and the others would all hoist him up in the air. So that's what Dad was doing, a huge smile on his face, and in his arms is a toddler: me. When I looked at that photograph, I hoped that maybe one day I could do something similarly impressive.

From a young age, Dad also made sure I always knew the rules of how to hold a firearm safely. For instance, you always kept a firearm pointed down. You always treated it like it was loaded. And you didn't hunt anything unless you were going to eat it. This was serious business. When Dad hunted deer in the wintertime, our entire family counted on that meat. One of the most important rules he ever taught me was: one shot, one kill. In other words, you never make an animal suffer. Ever. These rules are still so important to me, and I've since passed them on to my own son.

As I got older, my dad and my uncles started taking me along on their hunting trips, and these were such special times to me. I felt an attraction to being in the woods, almost like it was a part of me. If I was away from it for too long, it felt like something was wrong. On those trips my uncles taught me a lot about situational awareness, and learning to read and understand nature. We would all split up, and I remember being fascinated by how easily they could navigate in the woods. Using just a compass, and the occasional logging road as reference, they could take off for miles and still meet you back at the truck right when they said they'd be there. It was unbelievable.

Eventually I started hunting on my own, and I'll never forget the time I caught my first rabbit—and neither will Dad. I was seven or eight years old, and it was first thing in the morning, because I loved getting up early and going hunting before school. I snared this rabbit exactly the way I'd always been taught, and was so excited that I ran back home at full speed, yelling so loudly that every other creature within a hundred yards probably took off. I ran into the house, completely covered in snow, and didn't even stop to take my boots off. "Dad! Dad! Dad!" I yelled, running up the stairs. I was holding the rabbit by the ears in my left hand, and blood was dripping everywhere.

For whatever reason, there was something wrong with the showerhead that morning, and Dad had to have a bath instead. When he heard me yelling, he didn't know what was going on, and thought something must've been really wrong. But then I burst through the bathroom door, and I thrust this dead rabbit in his face before he'd even had a chance to get out of the tub.

"Look! I got one!" I yelled, grinning from ear to ear.

To his credit, Dad just started laughing. Even though blood was dripping into the tub, and he ended up having to take a second bath just to clean himself off from the first one. I'm pretty sure he was late for work that day. But I'll never forget how excited he was for me in that moment—that I had accomplished something like that all by myself.

I know that not everyone agrees with hunting nowadays. But for a lot of people, all around the world, it's a critical way of life. As recently as two hundred years ago, if you didn't hunt, your family starved. These days, it's still a decision that everyone gets to make for themselves. For me, it wasn't really about killing things. It was about appreciating and respecting nature, and all the creatures that God gave us to feed ourselves with.

Plus, in Pictou County, hunting was a critical part of the fabric of family. It was a skill that was passed down from generation to generation, and it brought us all a little closer together. I wouldn't be the person I am today without it.

Having such a close family was a blessing to me. But it also came with a wake-up call, when eventually I discovered that not all families were as tight-knit as ours. One year, Dad made the Canadian shooting team, and went, along with Mom, to an international competition in Bisley, England. While they were gone, both of my sisters went to stay at an aunt's house. But I was allowed to go stay with my buddy Neil and his family. By coincidence, they were also British. And I quickly found out they had a very different way of doing things than I was used to.

Don't get me wrong, they were a loving family. But from the moment I stepped into Neil's home, everything felt different. The food they ate was different from what I was accustomed to. So was their way of organizing their days: I was used to living casually, and making plans as they came up naturally, whereas Neil's house was a lot more regimented. It scared me a bit. To that point, the only culture I'd ever been exposed to was within my own family. I'd never even really been away from my parents before. Even though Neil was still a good buddy, I missed my parents and my sisters very much. Everything in the house seemed cold and dark, and I remember thinking, *I never want to do this again*. From then on, my room, and especially my bed, gave me a sense of security and warmth that I never again took for granted.

Mom and Dad didn't know anything about this, of course. They had a great time on their trip and came home with a bunch of rolls of film showing off their adventures together. Dad told me that he got to shoot against Prince Andrew in the competition. (Prince Charles was there, too, cheering on his younger brother from the stands.) I was happy for him, even though my experience of the trip had been a lot different.

As I sat around waiting for my age to tick over from eleven to twelve, I started doing my research. First, I talked to one of our neighbours down on Fox Brook Road in Pictou County. Technically, he lived two miles away from us, but in the country, that counts as your neighbour. This guy's son, John, was an air cadet, and after learning that I was interested, he took me under his wing a bit, and told me all about what to expect if I joined. Of course, back then there was no Google, so any book-related research happened in a library. I went to ours and checked out every single book I could find that had anything to do with the military, and memorized as much of it as I could, just in case it would improve my odds of being accepted.

Finally, the calendar rolled back around to August, and my

birthday arrived. I was twelve. Immediately, I went and signed up to join 374 Squadron in nearby Stellarton. On the night of our first meeting, I was terrified. This was it. I was finally about to take the first step in my journey, and I didn't want to mess anything up. I'd even gotten a haircut to show I was serious. Because it was the '80s and all, my mom usually let my hair grow out a bit, but I'd taken it upon myself to make sure that it was nice and short that night. I also put on my best golf shirt and corduroys, in the hopes of looking the part. At the same time, I was small for my age—with the exception of my head, which was the same size it is now. More than one person referred to me as a human bobblehead. Someone else once told me I looked like a watermelon on top of a toothpick. I was hoping none of the other cadets would notice.

It was already dark outside when I got to the meeting, and there were a bunch of bugs buzzing around underneath the exterior lights. The meeting was in a blue split-level building, with a huge insignia on the front. I remember standing out front, one hand on the doors, thinking to myself, *This is it*. When I opened the doors, this musty old smell filled my nostrils. It was like walking into a piece of history. As soon as that smell hit me, I was sucked in. I knew I'd arrived.

And it was a good thing that I'd decided to take some care with my appearance, because the first thing I noticed in the meeting hall was all these people in their pristine uniforms. I was still nervous, but there was no time to think too hard about it. There were orders being given, and like everyone else I was expected to follow them.

It's funny how certain people you meet have an effect on

you that lasts a lifetime. That's what happened when I met Jim Bradbury. He served in the military, but by the time I met him at cadets he was a civilian again (I think he had a job at the post office)—so I couldn't call him captain, or sir, or anything like that. It was always just Mr. Bradbury. And when this guy spoke, no joke, the entire room stopped moving. He commanded our attention. He got us all in line, quick. There were a bunch of cadets returning for their second, third, or fourth years, but there was also a gang of us who were brand-new. I remember looking around at a couple of the other new kids and thinking, *That kid could use a haircut.*

Sure enough, a few minutes later, the dressing-down began.

"Get your hair cut!"

"Why is there dirt on your face?"

"You call those pants?"

"Brush your teeth while you're at it!"

Oh boy, did Mr. Bradbury give it to us. Up one side, and down the other. It didn't matter that it was the first night, or that some of us had just signed up earlier that day. But at the same time, none of what he said was meant in a malicious or mean way—just a military way. You learned not to take it personally.

That first night, we received our orientation. We talked about flights, and ranks, and of course we all got to meet Captain Stevenson and the lieutenant. I was so excited to even be in the same room as them. But I noticed that everybody, no matter who they were or what their rank was, kept one eye and one ear on Mr. Bradbury the whole time. It was obvious that he was an accomplished man who commanded respect.

Once orientation was over, I filled out a form listing my hobbies and interests, and made sure to tell them about my experience hunting, fishing, and playing sports.

From there, I started attending meetings every week. At first, it was a bit awkward. I was enrolled and all, but I didn't really feel like I belonged until I got my uniform. Finally, one week they handed a stack of folded clothes to me. I'll never forget that moment. I brought the uniform home and unfolded it all on my bed, unable to stop staring at it.

How proud I was—even though it was obvious at a glance that none of it fit. The entire uniform needed to be altered, pretty dramatically, in order to fit my scrawny frame. I'm sure Mom's sewing skills were pushed to their limits. But I didn't care, and neither did she, once she saw how happy it made me.

My favourite part was the boots. Now, in the military, your boots are supposed to be like mirrors. And the only way you can take a new pair of boots and make them shine like that is through pure elbow grease: a can of black shoe polish, a rag, and a million circles. It's hard work, but to this day, I love shining boots. Much later in life, when I served as an honorary colonel at CFB Greenwood in west Nova Scotia, I kept my boots mirrored the entire time. Because even then, I was thinking back to my very first cadet meeting, and the first time I saw Captain Stevenson's boots. No exaggeration, they were like *glass*. You could use the reflection on those things to brush your teeth. He used to tell us, "If you're going to lead men, you have to lead by example." And that started with the uniform.

Once my boots were as shined up as I could possibly

make them, I was told that all of us cadets were going away for the weekend. The plan was to pile into an army bus and head off for three hours to visit a squadron in Newcastle, where we would be billeted, participate in a military parade, work on our drill exercises, and at the end have a dance. It was that last part that scared me more than the rest of the schedule combined. I had no clue how to dance. Plus, I was already self-conscious about being a tiny kid with a head so big that it basically had its own atmosphere. (In the end, nothing horrible happened. I just stood in the corner, terrified, the entire evening.)

But air cadets teaches you a lot about yourself, sometimes in unexpected ways. It gives you confidence in who you are—and not just your appearance, but your entire personality and identity. I've been an introvert from a young age, and cadets was the first thing that helped me come out of my shell, and to walk a little taller. Slowly, I started to take pride in who I was. My boot shining even got better over time—which was useful, because one of the mean things we used to do to each other was "accidentally" step on your buddy's boot, which would smudge the mirror so badly you'd basically have to start over. Some of the older cadets literally came to blows over this, because it took forever to get those boots up to snuff. It was a point of pride for all of us. If you were able to get your boots that shiny, it showed that you cared about your uniform, and that showed discipline.

I tried to distinguish myself in other ways, too. One of the things we worked on in that first year was rifle shooting. They asked if any of us had experience, and my hand shot straight up. I told them how my dad shot competitively, and about my own experience in the woods near our house. Once they'd seen what I could do, they asked if I'd be willing to teach the other cadets what I'd learned. At the time, I wasn't sure why they were asking me that, since they all knew a lot more than I did. It's only now that I realize it was a test of leadership. Luckily, I didn't hesitate. I stepped right up and said, "No problem." So over the next few weeks, in a classroom at the squadron headquarters, I taught the other cadets everything I knew.

At the end of my first year, all the cadets came together again for a wrap-up party. We did some more drills, and reflected on the year we'd had together. We also celebrated those cadets who had graduated and were moving on to basic training, which was a special occasion to witness. That's when Captain Stevenson gave me some more good news: I was being promoted to corporal. On a flight, corporals are basically second in command, behind the flight sergeant, and a cadet usually doesn't receive a promotion like that until at least well into their second year. It was a big deal, and I was blown away. My dad was there with me, and he couldn't believe it, either.

In case it isn't clear enough how much I loved cadets, I gave up my entire summer to go away to an air cadet camp. This was the first time I'd been away from home since my parents' trip to England, when I was stuck at Neil's house, and it was also the furthest from home I'd ever been. But this time was different because it was my idea. When I first applied to the camp, I was told it was full, which broke my heart. But a few days later, Captain Stevenson called me at home and said, "There's an opening. Do you still want to come?"

My heart started beating in double time. "Yes, sir," I told him.

He told me to be at the train station in Stellarton the next day, in full gear. "You're going to Greenwood," he said.

As soon as I got off the phone, I started rushing around to get my gear together. When I got to the Stellarton station, I hopped onto the train with another cadet who must've received a similar last-minute phone call. I'd never been in public in my full uniform before, and it was such a rush. Even though I was a very small piece in the huge puzzle that was the Canadian military, I still felt connected to the overall institution.

At one point we had to switch trains, and we were told to go for lunch at a nearby sea cadet camp while we waited. This was an even bigger camp than the one we were heading to, and it felt like the mess hall alone was the size of a Walmart. Inside were endless tables full of sea cadets—except for me and the other kid who was with me. We instantly felt out of place, and that feeling was confirmed when the sea cadets started cooing at us, like pigeons. It was meant to be a form of light hazing, I guess, but I just laughed.

Once we got to CFB Greenwood, there were four bunks per room. Again, it was full of that musty old smell that I grew to love. We settled in for the night, and first thing the next morning, just after 5 a.m., the whole building suddenly started to shake. I had no clue what was going on, but the other cadets treated it like it was no big deal. It turned out the barracks were right by the end of the runway where aircraft took off every morning. I later learned these planes were called Lockheed CP-140 Auroras, which some people call "submarine hunters," and which C-130 pilots joke is actually a C-130 with its engines upside down. None of those names meant anything to us at the time, though. We just knew them as the planes that woke us up every morning for the next two weeks.

The main thing we learned at camp was basic training. It was a little different back then than it is now—hopefully for the better because we're always trying to improve over time. Back then, we had to do drills on the hot tarmac in 38°C. I was sweating like crazy, and other cadets were passing out left, right, and centre. It was intense. But I learned so much in those two weeks: about leadership, about discipline, and also about friendship. That's where I started to understand that everybody has a story to tell. We all have experiences and perspectives that inform who we are as people, and how we understand the larger world around us. Years later, this would help me as an artist. When I write songs, I find myself thinking back to conversations I've had with people over the years, hearing about their experiences, and trying to put some of those moments and feelings to music.

When September rolled back around, my promotion kicked in, and I entered my second year of cadets as a corporal. With the new rank came new prestige, but also new expectations. I noticed the younger cadets looking up to me. My rank was respected all around, and I loved the added responsibility that came with it. Everything about the situation was perfect. I felt like my dream was finally starting to come true.

One thing that stands out about my second year was all the parades we attended. So many parades—and none larger or more significant than the one at the end of the training year, on July 1. Canada Day has always been a very important day for me, and a lot of that importance can be traced back to those early cadet marches. People used to come from miles away to watch our Canada Day parade, which featured pipe bands and military bands playing their hearts out. The first time I got to march in that parade as an air cadet, I was so proud I thought I was going to explode. I realized, though, that marching in a parade is a lot less fun than watching it. As a spectator, you get to relax in a lawn chair. Marching, on the other hand, involved hours of organized marching on hot pavement and some very sore feet afterwards. But I never regretted it. Every single time I put on the 374 Squadron uniform, it was with nothing but pride.

At the same time, I had an unexpected opportunity in music, when I found out that a band of older kids who epitomized '80s rock were looking for a new lead singer. These guys were decked out in spandex from head to toe, with the big Platinum Blonde hair to match, and I decided I would audition. I loved the music just as much as they did, but there were two problems: I didn't look the part, and my voice had recently changed. When I showed up to the audition in a basement in New Glasgow with a brush cut, wearing a golf shirt and corduroys, the band members were skeptical. Then, when I launched into Van Halen's "Panama," I had to sing it an octave lower than David Lee Roth in the original. The band played along with me for a few bars, then stopped and looked at each other.

"Uh . . . that's not how you sing it," one of them said.

"That's how *I* sing it," I said apologetically. "My voice is too deep now."

They consulted with each other, then turned back to me. "We're sorry," one of them said. "But we really need someone who can hit the high notes. Thanks anyway for coming."

My audition ended up lasting a grand total of less than a minute. I went back outside and flagged down my dad, who hadn't even gotten to the end of the block yet, and we drove back home together. Dad just looked over at me and said, "Got that out of your system, did you?"

I nodded along with him, disappointed. But I knew my true place was in cadets—or at least I thought it was.

After my second year, I opted out of cadet camp in favour of my first real job: running the fish station at my local McDonald's. It was a great way to earn some money and gain experience, but let's just say it's not a coincidence that to this day I've never eaten a Filet-O-Fish.

When it was finally time to start getting ready for school and cadets that fall, I started not feeling so well. It was strange. I didn't feel sick, exactly, but I also didn't feel right. I also started getting incredibly moody. Mom or Dad would ask me to do something, and I would snap—and not just because I was a teenager, either. I wasn't normally like that. Usually I was a respectful and polite kid who was guarded with my words. I wanted everyone to like me, and I always had a smile on my face. But suddenly my moods were swinging all over the place, and something was driving it. I just couldn't figure out what.

On my fourteenth birthday, I celebrated the fact that I'd been in cadets for two full years. Things were going really well for me. I started attending meetings again that fall, even though I still wasn't feeling quite right. Meanwhile the weather was turning colder, and as we got into December, one morning Dad asked me to come outside and help with chores. He wanted me to carry some armloads of wood into the house, which was something I did all the time. But this time, I was absolutely exhausted afterwards, and needed to drink tons of water just to feel normal again. That night I hardly got any sleep because I had to keep getting up every hour to pee. I didn't know it, but I was exhibiting all the common characteristics of type 1 diabetes.

Dad figured it out before I did. As the chief tech at the Aberdeen Hospital lab in New Glasgow, he knew all the symptoms. Plus, his mom, Honey, was also a type 1 diabetic. It seemed to run in the family. At the same time, Dad knew that if he took me in to get a blood test, I would have to stay in the hospital for at least a week. And Christmas was only a few days away. Instead, he and Mom made a secret plan to monitor my symptoms and make sure I could enjoy the holidays like normal. That's what they did.

But then, on Boxing Day morning, Dad took me in for testing at Aberdeen Hospital. A nurse there took a blood sample, and it was clear right away that my blood sugar was skyrocket high. The official diagnosis came shortly afterwards: I was a diabetic.

Immediately, I was admitted to the hospital and began receiving treatment. This happened on a Tuesday, and the whole time all I could think was: *I'm missing air cadet night*. Our meetings were held every week, even during the holidays, and in two years I'd never missed a single time. Now I was stuck in the hospital. I felt hopeless, and my mind started to wander.

*Will Captain Stevenson be mad at me for missing the meeting? Can I even stay in cadets if I have diabetes? Will they want me around? Are all my plans for the future ruined?*

Everyone around me was worried about my health, and I didn't really care. The only thing on my mind was whether I was about to be kicked out of the thing I loved more than anything else.

## Chapter Three

# STABBING THE ORANGE

O ver the next week and a half, I had a lot of time to think. It's funny: sitting there in my bed in the Aberdeen Hospital made me nervous—but at the same time, I had basically grown up in that same hospital. Dad was the chief technologist of the lab, and Mom had gone on to work for the head of surgery, a man named Dr. Cole, after leaving her job at the lawyer's office. Even as a very little kid, Dad had let me come in and hang out with all the lab techs, who would explain to me what each of these complicated pieces of equipment was used for.

This visit, however, was a lot less pleasant. When I was admitted, bright and early on Boxing Day, one of the first things they told me was that there was no room in the paediatric ward. Instead, I was taken up to the general men's ward. Even though I was fourteen, I was still a kid, but suddenly I found myself in this giant room with more than a dozen other patients, all of them fully grown adults. That first evening, it wasn't my diagnosis that freaked me out as much as my surroundings. It was pitch dark, aside from the blinking lights from some of the hospital machinery, and there were weird noises coming from every direction. Several of the men around me spent the entire night coughing aggressively. It felt like a horror movie. And because of my diagnosis, I wasn't allowed to eat anything—so I was hungry, terrified, and alone. All my old feelings of homesickness came right back to the surface. I didn't sleep a wink that night until my body finally gave up, and I passed out around 3 a.m. Until then I just lay there, staring at the ceiling, listening to these sounds, and praying. I asked God why He was letting this happen to me. It didn't seem right. What did I do to deserve this? As a teenager, it can be hard to see anything outside your own little bubble of reality. And I felt my bubble was closing in on me.

A few hours later, I was woken up by the nurses. And I've got to say, as much as people like to complain about health care in this country, the nurses and hospital staff I dealt with at Aberdeen were all on the mark. They took incredible care of me. That might have been partly because they knew my dad so well, and wanted to make sure his kid was taken care of. But they were so sweet, careful, and attentive that I'm pretty sure that's how they treated every single patient they worked with.

Along with their bedside manner, however, came some cold truths about my new reality as a type 1 diabetic. In Canada, we measure glucose levels in the blood with a unit called millimoles per litre (or mmol/L). The normal level for a person who isn't diabetic is anywhere between 4.6 to 6.5 mmol/L, depending on what you've eaten. On the morning I was admitted to hospital, my blood sugar was in the mid-40s. That is dangerously high. At that level, your organs are being damaged, and bad things can happen in a hurry.

If you don't have any experience with type 1 diabetes, let me back up a little and explain how it works. It all begins with an organ in your digestive system called the pancreas, which does a lot of essential stuff. One of the pancreas's important tasks is using its eyelet cells to create insulin, which is like a bridge that carries sugar from your blood into nearby cellular tissue. This is a critical process in your internal biology, but my body can't do it. My pancreas doesn't have any eyelet cells, and so can't produce insulin. Well, if there's no insulin, there's no bridge—and if there's no bridge, then my blood has no choice but to hold on to all that glucose, which makes the blood thicker. This causes my kidneys to start working overtime, pulling out all the water they can, trying to dilute the blood back to its normal consistency. My liver gets involved, too. This all puts immense strain on my body, and if that keeps up, it isn't long until everything has gone to hell in a handbag.

The first part of my hospital education was getting a crash course in what type 1 diabetes is, and how it affected my body. The second part was learning how to treat it. Because my body couldn't produce insulin on its own, I would have to learn how to take insulin externally, either through a needle or pump. But first, just to be safe, the hospital staff made me wait an entire twenty-four hours without food *or* insulin, to see whether my blood sugar could come back down to normal levels on its own. They wanted to be absolutely sure of their diagnosis before giving me external insulin for the first time. I appreciated the level of caution, but at the same time I was desperate for food. And when they finally let me have breakfast, it seemed like a cruel prank: a tiny portion of scrambled eggs, an equally tiny piece of toast, and a glass of water. That was it. Meanwhile, the nurses kept taking my blood, and checking, checking, checking. And their diagnosis, when they finally made one, turned out to be right on the money.

This was a lot for a fourteen-year-old to process, but in the back of my mind, I remembered that I knew a type 1 diabetic: my nanny. My dad's mom, Honey, had been a diabetic for as long as I could remember. When I visited that little old coal mining house and watched her bake a never-ending succession of pies and buns, she used to have to pause every now and then to test her blood sugar. Back then, the test where you draw blood by pricking your finger hadn't been invented yet (and it's already outdated today). The only test she had access to was by peeing on a special strip, which would show a colour that would tell you roughly where your blood sugar was. Then you would take the appropriate amount of insulin, based on that colour, to get your blood sugar back to normal. At least, that's how it was *supposed* to work. It was far from a perfect science, and there were times I could tell that even taking her medicine properly was exacting a toll on my nanny's health. She also didn't have disposable syringes. Instead, after every single use, she had to boil her glass syringe to clean it. And her insulin was the original stuff, made of beef and pork, which had a smell you would never forget. I know I haven't.

Technology had come a long way from urine strips and pork stink by the time I was diagnosed, thank goodness. For my first blood sugar test, I just took a small lancet, pricked my finger with it, put my blood onto a different kind of strip, and inserted it into a machine, which then told me my exact blood sugar level, down to a couple of millimoles. It was a much more precise way of measuring blood sugar levels, and also avoided the whole, you know, having-to-pee-onto-something part of the process. Then I would take my insulin based on that.

Now let me tell you about what diabetics call *the roller coaster*, and it's not a fun one. As an example, let's say your blood sugar is 15 mmol/L, and you know it's supposed to be somewhere between 4.5 and 6.5. To get it down, you take insulin—but how much? The truth is, you guess. It's an educated guess, but still a guess. For me, if I take one unit of insulin, my blood sugar will drop 2 millimoles. So as a teenager, figuring out how to do this for the first time, I learned I needed to take five units of insulin to drop from 15 mmol/L to that sweet spot of around 5.

The thing is, despite all the advances in technology since my nanny's day, it still isn't a perfect science. Even after I take my five units of insulin, sometimes that might pull my blood sugar down a little too low. And if that happens, my brain starts to panic, because now it's convinced it isn't receiving enough sugar to function properly. Time to counteract in the other direction, which, in my case, means I start eating like a madman. But the roller coaster is *still* not over, because it doesn't take all that much eating to ingest the ideal amount of sugar, and so by the time my brain has stopped panicking, I've usually eaten way more than I needed to. Which means—you guessed it—my sugar is once again too high. It's called the roller coaster because diabetics are always going up one hill, and then down another. I have another phrase for this never-ending process: *chasing the dog's tail*.

Another complicating factor is that there are actually two different kinds of insulin: long-acting and short-acting. When I was first diagnosed, we called them *lente* and *Toronto*, respectively. I'm not sure why they were called that, although Frederick Banting and Charles Best—the two doctors who invented insulin back in the 1920s—were both Ontarians. They were fascinating men, relentless in their work, and Dr. Banting was ex-military, too. I'd have loved to have been there the moment they finally figured it out and treated their very first patient, a little boy who was dying. Because until that point, diabetes was a death sentence. If I'd lived a century ago, I would be dead by now. I hate to say it so bluntly, but it's true. So I'm very grateful to Dr. Banting and Dr. Best. Without them, I wouldn't be here today, and neither would a bunch of other folks.

Anyway, learning to balance these different forms of insulin was a whole different challenge. Every morning I would calculate how much lente to take to get me through my school day, while also considering things like eating lunch, which would of course push my blood sugar up. To help with that calculation, I also had to measure my food to make a better guess at exactly how many calories I would be eating. But right when I woke up, I also had to take my Toronto insulin, which kicked in immediately, and created that bridge for whatever carbohydrates I was eating for breakfast. Basically, it involved a lot of math, and a lot of trial and error. Lying in that hospital bed, I had no idea any of this was in my future.

On day three in the hospital, I was told I was moving. Great! I was headed to the paediatric ward, where I would finally be around kids my own age. But before that could happen, one of the nurses said that I first needed to learn how to give myself a needle, so I could administer my own insulin. I don't remember this nurse's name, but I will never forget her. She was an older woman who had been in the field for a long time. She was a total sweetheart, but also a believer in tough love and getting to the point quickly.

So there I was, sitting in my bed in my hospital gown, looking dapper, I'm sure. The nurse came in with an insulin needle on a stainless steel hospital tray, alongside an alcohol swab and an orange.

*That's interesting*, I thought to myself when I saw the piece of fruit. I had thought I was getting a lesson, but maybe I was going to get a snack out of it, too.

"Okay, kid," the nurse told me, "today we're going to learn how to use an insulin needle." She proceeded to explain that the rind of an orange is a close approximation for human skin. She cleaned the orange with the alcohol swab, drew up some saline into the needle, and stabbed the needle into the orange. Then she injected the saline and pulled the needle back out. Once it was done, she turned to me and said, "Now you do it."

As she was showing me this procedure, I kept telling myself that once I got through it, I would be able to move to the paediatric ward. I decided to get this over with as fast as possible. Before I could second-guess myself, I grabbed the needle from her, drew up the saline the same way she had, and stabbed the needle into my leg.

"There!" I said with a smile.

The nurse looked at me with absolute horror on her face. "No!" she yelled. "You're supposed to inject it into the orange, not *yourself*."

For a minute she seemed like she was panicking, as if I had just given myself an infection on her watch—and the site of the needle stung like a bugger, I can't lie, because there was still some orange juice left on it from her demonstration. But after a few seconds she started laughing.

"Well, kid," she said, "you may not be that smart, but you're brave, I'll give you that."

And off we went to the paediatric floor.


When I talk to people about type 1 diabetes, one of the things I try to explain—especially to parents of children who have just been diagnosed—is that a lot of it is psychological. I know that sounds weird, because we treat it physiologically, with actual medicine, as well as with regular exercise, diet, monitoring, and so on. These things obviously work. But one factor we sometimes overlook is the psychological effects on the patient. Being a kid is already hard enough, and to have your entire life suddenly turned upside down—being told what you can and can't eat, and that you now have to live your life with almost military discipline—is extremely difficult on top of that.

For me, I was mostly concerned about getting back to air cadets. By being in the hospital, I was missing a cadets night for the first time ever. With each passing day, I started to panic a little bit more. *I gotta get back*, I thought. *I can't screw this up*.

One thing that helped me feel normal was getting to be around kids my age again. There was another guy in the paediatric ward named Peter, who had also been recently diagnosed as a diabetic. We ended up sharing a room, and discovered we had a lot in common: we both loved *Star Wars* and *Gremlins*, which had just come out, and we were both big fans of stand-up comedy. On our first night together, we stayed up late, excitedly talking about how my parents had promised to bring in a VHS player so we could watch movies together. Finally, I decided to turn in for the night. I was looking forward to a good night's sleep, but nope: every two hours a nurse would still come in to check on my vital signs, my blood sugar, or something else.

The good news was that I was allowed to eat again. Now, to be clear, it wasn't the best food, or the biggest portions, but I would devour absolutely anything I could get my hands on. This included dessert—and I am using the term *dessert* loosely. In fact, it was sugar-free Jell-O, which is terrible in just about every way. But I was so hungry I choked it down anyway. This came after a generous helping of celery, which I could eat without fear because it didn't trigger my blood sugar roller coaster, plus as much water and as many ice cubes as I could eat.

Over the next few days, my blood sugar continued to stabilize, and I started feeling better. When the lows came, as they inevitably did, my treatment was a glass of orange juice. I realized that it's quite difficult to have someone else treat my diabetic episodes. I'm the one experiencing a mental panic, but I can't describe it properly to anyone who's not also currently feeling it. In other words, it's not a mind-over-matter thing; it's learning to understand that my mind is actually mistaken.

So, no matter how much juice I pounded back, my brain kept chanting, *More, more, more*. But it took time for that sugar to get into my system, and I had to wait for it to take effect without overdoing it. It was—and is—a battle with my thoughts, every time.

Peter was going through the exact same thing as me. And having someone else there sharing that experience really helped. I was no longer by myself, in a dark room, surrounded by scary adults, with no idea of or context for what was happening to me. Peter and I were in this together. At the same time, in quiet moments, my fears would still slip back in—specifically, that every day I was in the hospital was another day I wasn't at air cadets. At times it felt like my entire future was up for grabs. I remember saying to my dad, "You've got to get me out of here. I have to get back." He asked me to be patient, and promised it would only be a few more days.

Visits from my family also cheered me up. It was great seeing my parents, and Cynthia and Mylissa were such an important part of what I now understand was my support team at the time. Sometimes support doesn't mean doing anything in particular—it meant the world to me just to know that my sisters were there for me, and rooting for me to figure this thing out. I remember Dad trying to keep my spirits up by reminding me that his mom was a type 1 diabetic, too. "It's going to be okay," he told me. "Now you're just like Nanny. She takes care of herself and so can you."

On one particular night, my sisters were off somewhere with a babysitter, and Mom and Dad finally made good on their promise to set up a movie night. Peter was there, too, of course. The hospital staff rolled in the TV and VHS player, and my parents asked us what we wanted to watch. Peter and I were unanimous: Eddie Murphy's *Raw*.

Murphy was one of our favourite comedians and actors, and this was his second big stand-up comedy special. We'd heard it was hilarious, and we were so excited to finally be able to see it. Now, if you've seen *Raw*, then you already know that it lives up to its title. Oh my goodness, were Mom and Dad embarrassed to have to sit through this incredibly foul-mouthed performance, even though Peter and I were howling with laughter the entire time. When I look back at it, this was the first time since I'd started feeling sick that I really felt like my old self again. And for a type 1 diabetic, that feeling of normalcy is not something that happens too often. You're always dealing with *something*. So that entire evening was a huge relief, being able to forget my diagnosis and all the uncertainties that came with it, even just for a couple of hours.

Soon I was feeling a lot better. So was Peter. One day we decided to commandeer a couple of wheelchairs and race each other down the hospital hallways. And the beautiful thing is that the nurses didn't stop us. In fact, I think they had some side bets on who was going to win each race. In retrospect, we might have been going a little stir-crazy. But that's natural, I think, when you lock a couple of fourteen-year-olds up in a little hospital room with no other outlets for their energy.

At long last, I was discharged. I breathed a gigantic sigh of relief as I walked through the front doors—or, rather, wheeled, since I insisted on taking my lucky wheelchair out for one last spin to the car.

What I didn't realize, though, was that when I got back

home, it was like the hospital all over again. Because Dad knew all about diabetes, he immediately implemented all those techniques in our house. From that point forward, my entire relationship to food changed. My sisters got to keep eating whatever they wanted, but everything I ate now had to be measured down to a fraction of an ounce. There was no more idle snacking of any kind. Oftentimes I had to stop eating even though I was still hungry. And if I came downstairs in the morning and saw a pillow on the kitchen table, that meant Dad was going to draw blood. He was checking my haemoglobin A1C, which is a measurement of your blood glucose over a three-month period. It was tough to get used to, but I'm so grateful now for my parents' commitment, because it forced me to take my health seriously. My diabetes was so tightly controlled that any side effects I encountered were minimal compared to those of a lot of other people my age.

Socially, it was even tougher. I would go to birthday parties, and while everyone else sat down to enjoy a nice piece of cake, I could only eat an apple. That sort of thing plays with your mind, and makes you feel isolated from the rest of your peers.

I was happy to be home again, but of course the main thing I was excited for was my return to air cadets, where I was intent on proving that I was still as committed as ever. When I got to that first meeting, though, I was immediately pulled aside and directed to the captain's office. Inside was the captain and the second lieutenant, and they asked me to sit down. Captain Stevenson said, "We're really happy you came back. But I'm afraid I have some bad news."

I froze in my seat. The first thing that jumped to mind was

that they were going to strip me of my rank. I knew I'd missed a meeting, so I figured I might be penalized, but I didn't think the punishment would be *that* serious.

But no. The captain held eye contact with me and continued. "Now that you've been diagnosed as a type 1 diabetic, there are two things you need to know," he said. "One, you can never be in the air force, and two, you will never fly an airplane."

## Chapter Four

# A TASTE OF MEDICINE

After that fateful night at cadets, I went back home and talked things over with Dad.

"You've got to be realistic, son," he told me as we sat next to each other on the couch. "There are a lot of things you're not going to be able to do anymore, and that's just the way it is."

I knew Dad was doing what he thought was best for me. It was a tough-love approach. Most of the time, he was a very loving parent, who never shied away from hugging and kissing us, or telling us how much he loved us. But in this situation, he knew what it meant to be a type 1 diabetic—because he grew up the son of one. He knew, from hard experience, what his mom could and couldn't do. He wanted me to be ready.

But I couldn't accept it. There was something stirring inside me that said, *No. This is not going to happen to me.* It seemed so unfair, just because I had this condition, that I couldn't be in the air force. That I couldn't fly an airplane.

That I couldn't be anything I wanted to be. In the days and weeks that followed, I remember looking around, as hard as I could, to find a famous person—any famous person—who had type 1 diabetes and was succeeding at life anyway. But I never found anyone, and so had to keep going on my own.

In thinking back on it, I was only fighting myself. Deep down, I realized my dad was right. My dreams were gone. I was never going to fly a plane. From that point forward, I knew on some level that my future was now going to be an endless succession of measuring my food, testing my sugar, and taking my insulin. I was a type 1 diabetic now, and I was going to have to get used to that fact.

But it was a difficult adjustment process. And if left to my own devices, I wasn't going to do any of it. As a fourteen-year-old, I wasn't interested in testing my sugar every day. Are you kidding? I was a teenager in the throes of puberty. I was already going through all kinds of confusing changes, I was told my dreams were no longer possible, and on top of that, I had to do all this extra stuff—just to live? Just to get by? No thank you.

The situation sucked. And, honestly, it still sucks to this day. I was recently asked to meet with the parents of a ten-year-old boy who was just diagnosed, and the kid was refusing to do anything for his own treatment. It was too much work, and overwhelming, and he was embarrassed, to boot. I could relate, even though it had been forty years since my own diagnosis. No matter how motivated you are, sometimes it just feels impossible to build up the willpower. And that's something the medical world has got to wrap its head around. I'm not alone in thinking this way. I've talked to hundreds of medical personnel over the years, and most of them agree that we need to consider the psychological effects this diagnosis can have on patients, especially young ones.

As always, I was grateful that my parents were there for me in my time of need. And my dad's tough-love regimen actually paid off, because it got my back up a little. After our conversation that first evening, I felt pissed off, which was exactly what I needed. There was no point feeling sorry for myself. I had to do something about it. And when Dad said all that stuff to me about being "realistic," I instantly got defiant. *Oh yeah? You're telling me I can't do all this stuff anymore? Well I'll show you* exactly *what I can and can't do.*

That was the moment I made my next big decision about my future, and once again it became clear in my mind instantly. I couldn't barge my way back into cadets. Fine. So instead of flying planes, I was now going to pursue a new career path: as a doctor. And not just any kind of doctor, either. I was going to become an endocrinologist, which is the kind of doctor that specializes in diabetes. If this stupid disease was going to take my dreams away from me, then I was going to learn every single thing I could about it—because I was not going to let it steal away the dreams of anybody else. I was going to find a cure.

Once again, I had no idea of the road that lay ahead of me, or what would be required for me to pull off something like finding a cure for diabetes. But I'm an impatient person by nature, and will generally do everything I can to achieve what I set out to do. I'll jump into the fire with both feet, and feel no regrets about it. I've always been that way. It probably used to drive my family crazy; I *know* it drives my wife crazy now. But I knew there was no way that God was teasing me: letting me develop this love of flying, and then snatching it away from me. There must have been a reason. Clearly, there was a different path I was meant to walk down instead.

When I told my parents about my new dream, they were both excited. Especially Dad. He thought it was a great decision, and he really stepped up to make sure I was exposed to more information and knowledge about a career in medicine. He started bringing textbooks home with him from the hospital and talking more about his work: what he did that day in the lab, and what interesting patients he dealt with (while always being sure to not give away any identifying personal information). Those conversations helped ramp up my interest in medicine even more.

Back at school, my teachers had all been told ahead of time about my diagnosis. I've since heard horror stories about other kids facing all kinds of tough situations at school, like teachers who don't even know how to talk to them anymore because they're so worried about what would happen if the kid had a diabetic reaction in class. But I was lucky. My teachers at West Pictou District High School were all supportive of me after my diagnosis, and just great people in general. It was a blessing to be around adults who really cared about the kids they worked with. Even the principal, Dr. Gunn, always took the time to talk to us kids about how our days were going.

The teacher that stands out above all the others, however, was named Dorothy MacIntosh. We used to call her Sarge. If you walked into her math class, you knew you had to work hard, and that she was going to personally make sure that you did. A lot of kids didn't appreciate Sarge's commitment. They thought she was just mean. But I didn't. I could see past her tough exterior, and I understood how big her heart was, how much love she had for her students, and how badly she wanted all of us to succeed. I hated every second of her class, and yet I learned so much from it. Once, when I was growing especially frustrated at a calculus assignment, she told me, "Take your time, Freddy. Don't let the problem overwhelm you. Break it down into pieces." That was a life lesson, even though I didn't realize it at a time. Sarge turned out to be a huge influence on me learning how to dig down and find that determination and that drive, which spilled over into other areas of my life, including how I handled my diabetes.

With the support of my teachers, I was quickly able to get back to my studies, where I was now motivated to work twice as hard as I had before. I studied for so long, in fact, that I ended up giving myself an ulcer. That's how much pressure I was putting on myself. Dad told me to relax, and to just focus on doing my best, whether that was a 100 or a 70 or a 50. But I knew I needed top-notch marks to get into medical school, and I was determined to get them by any means necessary.

Academics weren't all bad, though. I liked biology and chemistry well enough. And, to my great surprise, I discovered I really enjoyed drama—especially our class musicals. In one memorable performance, I played the role of Cyrano de Bergerac, complete with enormous fake nose. I was a shy kid in other parts of my life, but I found that when I stepped onto that stage, I felt like I was stepping into a different world. It was such a liberating feeling. I got to put on a costume and pretend that I was someone else, even if only for a couple of hours. The moments *before* I stepped onstage were always terrifying, but I knew that once I got out there, parading around under the bright lights in my gigantic fake nose, my fears would disappear and I could truly relax.

I also joined the debate team, and in grade twelve, I ran

for grad class president. At first, I was hesitant, since I wasn't a natural politician, and also because there didn't seem to be a lot of benefits to the job, only added headaches and obligations. But once again, that internal drive kicked in, and for whatever reason I ended up winning. Somehow I had managed to give my speeches and talk to people about my plans, and I guess I convinced enough of them that I was the right person for the job. To this day, I still don't quite believe it happened. But I took the position very seriously and worked hard to do right for my classmates.

But one of my best memories of high school was joining my first band: an '80s-rock cover band called Reaction. I'm still such a fan of the songwriting and the melodies of music from that era. There's something special about it. We played all the hits: everything from Pet Shop Boys to Glass Tiger to Bryan Adams to Cinderella. I was the guitar player, drawing on the skills I'd been slowly teaching myself since the first time I strummed one of my parents' old guitars, sitting on our ugly green couch, at the age of five.

Now, I said this was my first band, but strictly speaking, that's not true. Way back when I was in grade five, me and two other buddies joined up to play two songs at our school's variety show. I was the piano player, which was an odd choice, because I'd lasted all of three weeks of lessons before quitting and had otherwise taught myself how to play by ear. Our first song was "The Rose," which was made famous by Bette Midler, and the other was "A Hard Day's Night" by the Beatles, where I switched over and played guitar. My gosh, it was so much fun. Technically, that was my very first live performance, and I've never really talked about it before. If you're reading this book, that's what we call an exclusive.

Anyway, my high school band Reaction played a couple of gigs around town, including a dance at another school in Westville. Most of the time, we just made a lot of racket practicing in Mom and Dad's garage. But it sure was fun. That was the only thing on our minds at the time. We weren't too concerned with stuff like musicianship.

When it came time to plan our class graduation that June, the school asked me if I would perform a song with a friend of mine named Cheryl. We ended up doing a Dan Hill tune, and even though it came with the usual round of *Why am I doing this?* pre-show jitters, the performance went off great. I should also mention that those jitters are especially difficult for a type 1 diabetic, and can wreak havoc on your blood sugar, sending it way up or way down depending on the situation. Sometimes I'd have to grab a last-minute snack or take a final dose of insulin just before walking onstage, even though I felt like I was going to puke from nerves.

Despite that, I seemed to have an instinctive drive to put myself in those kinds of performance situations. I think it was the challenge itself that appealed to me. I didn't enjoy the feeling, but for some reason I had to do it.

Now, of course, I can see why. While my heart was set on becoming a doctor, the Lord had an entirely different career in mind for me—one that I knew nothing about at the time. But for me to be ready for it, I needed to have these experiences in front of an audience. I needed to be able to get past those feelings of anxiety, and those panicked thoughts of, *What am I doing up here? Everyone's looking at me. I don't know what to do!*

God's plans turned out to be perfect. I just didn't know it until it started to unfold in front of me, a few years later. But I'm getting ahead of myself.

## Chapter Five

# KING ARTHUR'S REPLACEMENT

After graduation, I set my sights on med school, and I got accepted to three different schools: Dalhousie, St. Mary's, and St. Francis Xavier. I liked that SFX was a smaller school, so I knew I would get more one-on-one time with the faculty. It was also only forty-five minutes from home, in Antigonish, which appealed to me as a homebody (my parents liked it for the same reason). Some people love the idea of going off to party thousands of miles away, but not me. Plus, as a diabetic, partying just wasn't an option; I tried it once and was as sick as a dog for days. Lesson learned.

I enrolled in St. Francis Xavier's pre-medicine program. This meant I didn't have to take a full undergraduate degree, and allowed me to bypass some of the courses that really didn't affect becoming a doctor. At the end of the second year, I could apply to med school. The flip side, however, was that to get all the required courses completed in time, I would have to take second- and third-year courses in my first year, and fourth-year classes in my second year. Of course, I didn't realize any of this when I signed up. It took me a few days to really understand that I'd bitten off more than I could chew. At the same time, I was used to trying things that scared me. So I dug in—hard. While all the other new students were out partying and letting loose, I sat in my dorm room, studying and giving myself more ulcers in the process.

Interestingly enough, the hardest classes I took at SFX were the ones I did the best in. I think that's because those are the grades where I had to really earn every percentage point. One of those classes was physics, and another was math. (Thanks, Sarge!) My math professor at SFX was a priest named Father Charlie. He was so patient with us, and so giving of his time, and a brilliant thinker in his own right. By the time I was in my second year, Father Charlie had taught me statistics, calculus, and finally advanced calculus—where I shocked myself by getting 96 percent on my final exam. I'd never gotten a mark that good before, and I never would again. I took that as proof that I had the drive and determination to become a doctor after all.

I was proud of myself, and equally proud of the fact that I'd been able to do all this while living with type 1 diabetes. Because at that point, I was still figuring out what I could and couldn't do. I wasn't sure how the disease would affect my memory, or my ability to process information at that level and at that speed. When my sugar gets too high, for instance, I get tunnel vision and I can't really concentrate—what if that happened during an exam? These were hurdles I had to deal with that most of the other students really had no idea about.

After my first year of university, I went back home and landed a job in the maintenance department of the Aberdeen Hospital, where I cut lawns, picked up garbage, and worked whatever odd hours they asked me to. Sometimes that involved night shifts, and things could get a little creepy. Whenever I had to go down to collect garbage from the morgue, for instance, I used to carry a harmonica with me, and play it as I walked the halls, just to hear something.

One night I was on my way back out of the morgue, and the lights in the building turned off. There was a storm outside that evening, and suddenly it was pitch black. There was not a stitch of light anywhere. I was so scared that I literally could not move. I didn't have a flashlight, or a cell phone, so I grabbed my harmonica and started playing. I played that thing as loudly as I could, listening to the music echo off the morgue walls, until the lights finally came back on and I could get out of there. It was probably only a couple of minutes, but to me it felt like eternity.

No matter whether I was working in the hospital or back in class, the whole time I had my eyes set on med school at Dalhousie. But during my second year at St. Francis Xavier, I noticed a flyer put out by the university theatre, which was right behind my dorm. It said they were holding auditions for the musical *Camelot*. Once again, something inside me drove me to audition in the days before we all went home for the Christmas break. Partly I understood desires like this to be part of the good Lord's plan for me, and I knew enough to trust them whenever they came along. I ended up being cast as one of the lesser knights of the Round Table. The part came with a grand total of one line, which was a big deal to me then.

I was excited and went back to my parents' house to enjoy the holiday. A few days after I got there, though, I got a phone call from the university. It was the director of the show.

"The guy we cast as King Arthur has gotten sick," she said.

"He can't do the part. Would you be interested in auditioning to be his replacement?"

I just laughed. I was going to say no—but something in me said yes first. Another risk. Another chance to pursue this fascination I had with the stage and see where it led. Why not?

Back in Antigonish, I tried out and, wouldn't you know it, ended up getting the part. So all of a sudden I was going to be the star of a play that would run for eleven days. It was an incredible opportunity, and that mixture of terror and excitement carried me all the way to opening night.

There I was, sitting in my dressing room, in full tights and armour, with my sword across my lap. I felt like I was King Arthur himself. And as I heard the distant murmur of the audience taking their seats, I started praying: *Please, Lord, don't let me embarrass myself tonight. Let me remember my lines, hit my cues, and not mess up singing along with the live symphony that I can already hear warming up on that balcony*. It was my faith that really got me through those initial jitters, and eventually I was able to find the strength to walk through the curtains and transform myself into the King of the Britons.

Once I was actually on the stage, I was reminded of the immense talent of the rest of the cast, the director, and the crew, who were all so good at their jobs that it made for a natural, seamless experience. My costar was an exchange student from Scotland, and she had this talent, which is rare among singers, where, even when you listen to them sing a cappella, your mind fills in the gaps, adding instruments to the music when they aren't really there. I don't know if she pursued a career in music, but I hope she did. Being part of that production felt like I was stepping inside an actual story, and all I had to do was say my part. It felt like one continuous song.

I loved the feeling that being in the musical gave me. Not only was it new and exciting, but it was also the opposite of the feelings I had when I was studying, which was all pressure and stress. Despite my pre-show jitters, the theatre was a liberating place. I felt like I was my true self onstage. But at the same time, there was still a part of me that didn't want to recognize it—the part that was focused on becoming a doctor and saving the world. I wasn't ready to let my artistic side take over just yet.

Those eleven days in *Camelot* were amazing. And it turned out they were a big part of God's plan for me. Because in the audience at one of those shows were three musicians from a local rock band in Antigonish called Counterpoint. I knew who they were, because the group had already had some success. After the show, the drummer from the band approached me. He looked like the Maritime equivalent of Bon Jovi, with long blond hair, an open shirt collar, chains around his neck, and tight, ripped jeans. His name was Todd, but everyone called him Skippy.

"Hey, nice job tonight," he said, then cut to the chase. "Listen, our lead singer has had to step down. Would you be interested in auditioning to be his replacement?"

I was still fired up from the show and wasn't sure I'd heard him properly. "You're kidding, right?"

"Actually, no." Skippy grinned. He went on to explain that Counterpoint was looking to change genres, too: from rock to country.

That was interesting to me. Even at that age, country music had been part of my life for a long time—mostly through its connections to folk music. In fact, early country music was basically a bunch of folk songs with a twist. A lot of the music I've written over the course of my career falls into that category, too, technically speaking. I tend to gravitate towards story songs, whether I'm singing about family, love, faith, or even having a good drink every now and then. The storytelling always comes first.

I considered Skippy's offer and then said, "Yeah. I might be able to do that."

I don't remember what song I sang at the Counterpoint audition, but given their hopes of switching over to country, I have a hunch it was a Randy Travis song. Randy's music has had a huge influence on me over the years. When I was sixteen, my first vehicle was Mom and Dad's old Ford Tempo, and I used to drive around with Randy's album *Old 8x10* blaring from the cassette deck. I knew every word, and every vocal tic, on that record. At the time I thought it was all just for fun, but it turned out to be a huge asset, because I otherwise didn't have much training in how to sing a country song.

Being a good mimic was a real point in my favour. Doing my best impression of Randy Travis is what landed me the gig in Counterpoint, I'm sure. And it's also what gave me some early success once we headed out on the road for the first time. When people came to have a good night out at the bar, they wanted to feel as though they were listening to the real artist when they heard our covers. So my job wasn't just to be the lead singer of Counterpoint. It was to be able to sound like Dwight Yoakam, Randy Travis, Alan Jackson, Garth Brooks, Clint Black—the list went on.

I started rehearsing with Counterpoint during that spring semester. We'd rehearse once or twice per week, and it was a bit tough, trying to juggle my classwork with this new music thing. But I was determined to make it work, because I really enjoyed it. All of us band members became like brothers in that time, and our girlfriends became friends, too. It was a real bonding experience. We felt like one big family of music.

Music was also a perfect release from the grind of studying. Truth be told, when I wasn't with the band, I was in a bit of a dark place. My decision to become a doctor was weighing down on me in a way that it hadn't before. I did truly want to pursue medicine—but at the same time, that decision had come from a place of obligation. I felt I *needed* to help other people, and that feeling felt like more of a burden with every passing week.

When I was playing with the band, however, that weight of expectation just lifted from my shoulders. It was some of the most fun I'd ever had. Over time, we got pretty good, too. Our guitar player was Paul, a skinny guy with long, curly red hair that he used to tease the absolute snot out of—like the rock 'n' roll version of Carrot Top. On bass was Darren, who was quiet, kind, and extremely fit. Skippy was on the drums, and I sang. We would practice at Paul's place, where he'd turned his entire living room into a jam space, full of amps and gear and a complete drum kit. On top of singing, I also played this old semi-hollow Yamaha acoustic guitar. At our peak, we would rehearse for six to eight hours every day. It got so hot in Paul's house that, no joke, sometimes we would strip down and rehearse in our underwear—and by the end of the session we'd all be dripping with sweat anyway. That was how much we loved the music we were playing.

Eventually we decided it was time to head out on the road together and play a bunch of shows out of town. I was nervous to tell my parents that I was going to be gone most of the summer, but I assured them I would be back in time to start at Dalhousie Medical School. Mom and Dad agreed that it sounded like fun, and gave me their blessing. "Take the summer," Dad said. I could tell he was hesitant about where this strange new opportunity might lead, but he respected my desire to do things my own way. "Let loose, have some fun, and we'll see you in the fall."

Our tour was made possible thanks to our first manager, a guy named Doc Holiday. Doc was an American from Virginia, but he spent his summers in Pictou County and he was a friend of my parents. One night he came out to see Counterpoint play a dance at the Westville Curling Club, which I was familiar with, as I'd been the skip of my high school team and even taken us all the way to provincials. But during the warmer months the owners used to melt the ice and host events there. I remember there was a small turnout at our show that night. But after the show, Doc came over and introduced himself. He was a giant of a man, at least 6'4", with a big beard and smoky glasses so you couldn't see his eyes.

"You guys are real good," he said in a rough and gravelly voice, as if he'd just walked off the set of a John Wayne movie. "I'm gonna take you on the road and get you a record contract."

These were exactly the words we were hoping to hear. All of a sudden, it felt like our musical dreams were about to come true.

Sure enough, Doc started booking us gigs, and we were all so excited for our careers to be taking off that we said yes to the arrangement right away, without inspecting the financial side too closely. One of the things that came up early on was that we had to pay for and transport all our own production—so not just gear, but also the lighting and sound systems—to each show. None of us in the band were wealthy, and neither were our parents. We didn't even have part-time jobs, because we spent all of our free time rehearsing. So where was this money supposed to come from?

I was lucky, because I'd had the foresight to save some money from my earlier jobs. But even after I'd used up all of my savings, we still barely had enough to make our payments on the production, and had to scrape by as best we could. I'll never forget loading up the van for our first couple of gigs. It was an old, busted thing, with no side doors and no backseats. We stuffed our speakers and gear inside through the back, and then decided who among us would get to sit in the front, and who had to go ride with the amps. There were five of us in total: all four band members, plus our sound guy, Fabian. And the three of us who drew the short straws were forced to crawl into the back and lie down on top of the speakers like a bunch of human torpedoes. We drove that way from Pictou County, Nova Scotia, to a little town called Manitouwadge in Northern Ontario.

Back in those days, you played at each venue for a week, Monday to Saturday. Then on Sunday you'd travel to the next bar, and do it all over again. It can be grueling, thankless work, but we didn't care. At the end of that first set in Manitouwadge, we thought we were all that and a bag of chips. And by the time our week of gigs was up, something inside me had permanently changed. I knew that this was the plan God had for me. It was going to be music, and not medicine, that drove me from that point forward.

## Chapter Six

# LESSONS FROM
# THE ROAD

L ife on the road was a real shock to the system. You have
to remember, at the time we were still a bunch of teenagers who'd never really left Nova Scotia, aside from the odd
family vacation to Disneyworld. And now we found ourselves
squished inside a busted old van, driving twenty-four hours
straight to get to Manitouwadge, a little township in Ontario
that, until a few days earlier, we'd had no idea even existed.

Actually, our first official band road trip took even longer
than the maps suggested, because as soon as we crossed the
border from Nova Scotia into New Brunswick, we hit serious
highway construction, and traffic in both directions came to a
standstill. It was early summer, and unbelievably hot outside,
and the only air-conditioning our van had access to was the
old-school kind Papa used to call "2-80": two windows down,
80 miles an hour. (Not that our van could have gotten close
to 80.) Here, however, it was gridlock as far as the eye could
see. Nobody was moving. I was the driver, so at least I had a
proper place to sit. Skippy was next to me in the passenger

seat. But the rest of the guys were in the back, lying in a row on top of the gigantic Cerwin-Vega speakers we were carting with us to Manitouwadge. Not ideal travelling circumstances, to say the least, but I remember looking around and seeing huge smiles on all our faces. Why? Because we were real musicians, on our way to a real gig! Skippy was listening to his Walkman with headphones on, and he was having a great time, singing along to Bon Jovi—Skippy loved that man, and had the hair to match—and imagining the exciting things that lay in our shared future.

We were a little nervous, too, but those first shows in Manitouwadge were a fantastic introduction to life as a touring band. At the time, country rock as a genre was still coming into its own, and our repertoire included everything from Randy Travis to Tom Petty to John Cougar Mellencamp. Country rock wasn't the old, traditional country sound, but it wasn't rock music, either—it was this new combination of both. We learned as many of the top songs as we could, but we still had a long way to go as musicians. Fortunately, there's no better way to learn than on the job.

The people of Manitouwadge were lovely and welcoming. The band house, however, was not. When we opened the door to where we'd be living between shows, we discovered the beds didn't have sheets on them, and therefore nothing to disguise the dirty, stained mattresses underneath. Also, our toilet didn't have a seat on it, and the bathroom between the two bedrooms was missing its door. As we would soon discover, this wasn't an uncommon situation for band quarters. But at the time we didn't care. Just being on the road was good enough for us.

After a couple of shows in Manitouwadge, we packed our

gear back in the van and drove another twenty hours all the way up to Thompson, Manitoba. This time we were booked for two full weeks at a place called the North Star Saloon, inside the Thompson Inn. When we finally pulled up in front of the venue and stepped back out of the van, I had no idea where I was, but I couldn't believe how beautiful the scenery was. Summertime in Northern Manitoba is a special experience.

I can still vividly picture the stage of the North Star Saloon, not to mention the stuffed animal heads that lined the walls. But, if I'm being honest, a lot of those early shows are kind of a blur to me now, simply because we played so many of them.

One thing I do remember from those early days, however, was that every Saturday afternoon we hosted a jam session, where anybody from the audience could join us onstage. This was standard in the '90s, and it was one of the most entertaining things I got to do on the road, just because of how unpredictable it was. A half-drunk guy would stomp up onto the stage and say, "I wanna play Steve Earle's 'Copperhead Road,' and I wanna play it in F!" And we'd have to figure out a way to make it work. So we learned a whole pile of songs, just in case somebody requested them. You never really knew what people were going to be in the mood for, though obviously it was influenced by whatever was popular at the time. We played an awful lot of "Copperhead Road" when that particular tune was climbing the *Billboard* charts. But sometimes we'd also get old country requests, which I loved, because I grew up listening to that stuff. Having to play classics like "Rhinestone Cowboy" or "Ring of Fire" really helped build our repertoire. Over time we even added some of those songs into our shows, which I think gave us an edge over some of the other country rock bands out there. All in all, the band might've gotten more out of those Saturday-afternoon jam sessions than the people who came up to play with us did.

As we spent more time on tour, our musicianship improved and we really bonded as a band, which was great. But I can't deny that a feeling of loneliness started to creep in. For one thing, it was difficult to find things to do during the day. After playing a show and staying up until the early hours, the other guys in the band would all sleep in until noon, but I never could. Because of my type 1 diabetes, I had to be up at 7 a.m. to eat and take my insulin for the day. Those lonely hours started to weigh on me, and I really stopped taking care of myself the way I needed to.

Money was always tight, and we had to make what felt like a never-ending series of payments on our gear, the van, and a bunch of other associated costs. Once you deducted those expenses, the most we ever made during those years was around $50 per week. It sounds terrible, I know. And yet I use that story all the time with my kids, because that's how you know you truly have a passion for something. If you're willing to do that much hard work for little or no money, but you still wake up with a smile on your face, excited to see what the day will bring, that means you're on the right track.

In those days we all survived on Ichiban noodles and Kraft Dinner. I'd also pick up the cheapest cereal I could find, which, inevitably, was loaded with sugar. As a type 1 diabetic, you just can't do that stuff—and yet I did. I remember testing my sugar, at most, two times per day. Eventually I had to stop and say, *What the hell am I doing?* Testing twice per day gave me a rough idea of where my sugar was at. But I wasn't doing anything about it. I was even rationing my insulin so that I didn't have to spend any extra money, or, worse, borrow more from Mom and Dad, who were not happy when they learned about my little money-saving technique.

I did smarten up, in the end. But it took a while. I was your typical nineteen-year-old, and I thought I was bulletproof. As a type 1 diabetic, that's one of the worst things you can think. Interestingly enough, after working with a lot of other type 1 diabetics and their families over the years, I've discovered that most of them think the same way at that age. So maybe I was just par for the course.

From Thompson, it was on to Flin Flon, and a venue called the Paw. A lot of the towns Doc booked us to play were what you'd call secondary or tertiary markets—not the kinds of places where A-list bands usually visit. That meant that the venues weren't full-time concert halls, and usually had to serve multiple purposes. Well, one of the purposes of the Paw was to host adult female dancers—and they didn't stop working just because a band happened to be booked that week. During our time there we got used to seeing a dancer come on before our sets, and sometimes even between them. Especially the noon-hour shows.

Those first gigs at the Paw went really well, and not long afterwards we came back to Flin Flon to play another round of shows. We assumed we were playing the same venue, so we didn't look too closely at the details of the contract. But when we showed up at the Paw, there was another band setting up. We went outside to a pay phone and called up Doc long-distance to figure out what was going on.

"No!" he told us. "You guys aren't playing there again.

You're playing a new bar, and you're getting paid more money. Trust me, it's even better. You'll love it."

*A new bar? Fantastic!*

As it turned out, the bar we were booked at turned out to specialize in not country rock, and not even rock, but heavy metal. Oh man, people were not happy to see us walk in that door. We might not have looked like cowboys, but we definitely didn't look like headbangers. To tell the truth, we were a little scared. We were scheduled to play there for an entire week, and sure enough the first few gigs were bad. People would curse at us, or loudly get up and leave mid-song. We even talked among ourselves about cutting out early but decided: "No. We're stubborn—we're Nova Scotians. We are going to see this thing through."

So we kept playing. And wouldn't you know it, by the weekend, the place was jam-packed. We had won over the heavy metal crowd. You have to remember, Darren, Skippy, and Paul were versatile musicians, and could play *heavy* when they wanted to. So in the middle of our set, they'd tear into some Yngwie Malmsteen and the place would go wild. Then they'd go right back into another Randy Travis song and somehow the place would go wild *again*! That experience really taught us a lot about music, and how if you're willing to be positive and give people the benefit of the doubt, sometimes it all works out.

No matter what your science textbooks may have told you, time is not linear—at least, not when you're on tour. As a travelling musician bouncing between provinces and time zones, time can start to slide around in unpredictable ways.

There were many times I would wake up in a band house, not knowing where I was, and jumping onstage that night only to ask Skippy, mid-song, "What day is it?" You always knew when it was a weekend show because the crowds were much bigger. And Thursdays were usually ladies' nights. But for a lot of those early weeknights, the shows all started to blend together. In moments like that I started to ask myself a lot of questions—like, *Is this a good use of my time? Or am I just spinning my wheels?*

When the band first went out on tour, it was supposed to just be for the summer. After that, I was meant to come back home and begin med school at Dalhousie. Well, that didn't end up happening. We had enough success that summer to continue getting offered gigs into the fall, and we felt we had to keep accepting them, just to see where this road would lead. Really, we wanted to be the next Diamond Rio. We wanted a record deal, and to play sold-out shows across the continent. We wanted it all.

I thought back often to the conversation I had with my parents before that first tour, because I think Dad knew on some level that this was the end of my medical career, and he was clearly disappointed, even though he did his best to hide it. As a parent myself now, I get it. It's hard. You always want the best for your children, and my dad knew that life as a musician would be tough, whereas as a doctor, I could live a comfortable life and do so much good in the world. He'd really had to swallow his pride and let me go out there and make my own mistakes—if indeed music turned out to be a mistake. The truth is, you can never really know until you get out there and give it your best shot.

———

When we first signed with Doc Holiday, we didn't know much about the music industry. But we had to admit he did a great job booking us shows. Then one day he called us and said, "Okay, boys, it's time for you to do a record." Finally!

Now, this was back in the days when you recorded direct to tape. Real old-school record making. And once again, Doc had it all worked out. The plan was for us to record at a studio in Virginia, where he lived, so I borrowed Mom and Dad's K-car and the band headed to America.

We were set to record a single song: Van Morrison's "Tupelo Honey," a soulful country tune that had been a big hit when it was first released in 1972. The plan was this would be a radio single that we would then use to pitch ourselves to record labels. I don't know how we ended up settling on that particular record, but again it was probably Doc's idea. Either way, the session happened quickly, because it turned out the only thing we had to actually do was for me to record my vocals. The rest of the band members didn't play on the track; there were session musicians who had already recorded the other instruments by the time we showed up. This might sound unusual, but at the time was quite common, just because the studio is such a different animal than playing live.

What was most noteworthy about our first recording session was the motel we stayed in afterwards. Skippy and I were rooming together, which was usually how we split ourselves up when we couldn't all pile into one room. At bedtime, I locked the door—but I did not put the chain across the door. This turned out to be a critical mistake, because in the middle of the night, the hotel's cleaning lady snuck into our room and robbed us while we slept. Neither Skippy nor I had a credit card at the time, so everything we had on us was in cash. This woman found and took it all. And not just from our room, either. We learned afterwards that she had recently quit her job, and so on her last night went around and stole from as many rooms as she could get into.

Ever since I was a kid, I've always been a trusting person. I wanted to believe that people weren't mean or cruel for no reason, and that everyone's intentions came from a good place. So right away I started coming up with excuses for what this woman had done. Maybe she truly needed the money—maybe even more than we did. Skippy, on the other hand, didn't see things that way. When he woke up and realized what had happened, he charged out of the room and downstairs towards the office, all while wearing only his underwear. He was that angry about it. In the end, we got back home from Virginia a little more jaded than when we'd left. On the plus side, we had our first recorded song to show for it, even if, ultimately, it would never end up making it to radio.

From there, it was back on the road again. And for the next five years, we travelled from coast to coast, seeing as much of this beautiful country as we could.

I could fill an entire book just with wild road stories. One time we played a show in Atikokan, Ontario, and there was chicken wire covering the stage. It was like something out of *Road House*, and we just thought it was the coolest thing ever. Of course, it didn't dawn on us until our first set kicked off the reason *why* there was chicken wire covering the stage—and that was because the locals were known to throw beer bottles at whoever was performing on it. The bottles didn't always make it to the stage, but the beer inside sure did. The chicken wire gave us just enough traction to stay on our feet and continue playing. At the end of the evening, I remember having to wipe down literally every single piece of gear we owned. But we had to laugh because the beer wasn't being thrown in anger. It was just what they did in Atikokan, I guess.

That show was also significant because it was the first time I ever drank so much alcohol that I threw up. As in most places, the band's quarters were above the bar, and for whatever reason we decided to have a little party after our last set. I had only just turned nineteen, and I drank an entire mickey of Captain Morgan. Now, I know that for some people, that isn't a lot of booze. But for someone like me, who didn't drink that much at the best of times, it was plenty. I was so sick, and of course it completely threw off my sugar levels in the process. I learned my lesson from that one pretty quickly.

Another night we were onstage, this time in a venue and town I won't mention, and everything seemed to be going fine. Given the type of music we played, dancing was always a big part of our shows—it wasn't unusual to see the entire floor packed end to end with line dancers, all moving together as one big group. When a group of more than a hundred people all stomped their feet down at the same moment, the shock waves were so powerful that we could feel it from up on the stage. Well, on this evening an argument broke out right in the middle of the dance floor between a young couple. I watched it happen from the stage, and it was like it was happening in slow motion. The guy pulled his arm back, made a fist, and hit his wife so hard that she flew in the air backwards and landed, out cold, on her back. We were in the middle of a song, and I just stopped singing. The rest of the band came to a crashing halt behind me.

The way I was brought up is that anytime someone raises a hand against a woman—for any reason—you come to that woman's defence. It doesn't matter who it is, what they did beforehand, or any other details of the situation. Violence just isn't okay. And the rest of the boys in the band were raised the same as me. We were about two seconds away from jumping down into the crowd, but luckily a handful of other patrons had the same idea we did, and they grabbed hold of the attacker so quickly that I don't think his feet touched the ground again until he was thrown out into the street. Then someone else grabbed some ice for the poor lady's injury, and thankfully she was all right in the end. But that's an image I don't think I'll ever be able to forget.

Another time, at another show, there was this drunk guy who just kept trying to get up onto the stage. We didn't really have any security to speak of. You just trusted that people would behave themselves and enjoy the music. But this guy, man . . . he just had to be *that* guy. We tried to play through his antics, but eventually it was Darren, who usually had the patience of Job, who reached his wits' end first. He'd had enough. The next time this guy tried to rush the stage, Darren swung his bass guitar at him and knocked the guy flat. And wouldn't you know it? He stayed in his seat for the rest of the show and didn't cause any more trouble.

One time we were booked to play at a venue in Saskatoon that, sadly, isn't around any longer. From the second we walked in the door, we fell in love with this place. The servers and managers were all so kind and welcoming to us. Right away we felt like we were at home. It wasn't until we started playing that I noticed that every single person in the audience was Indigenous. That was fine by us, of course. I'd grown up around plenty of Indigenous folks in Nova Scotia, where the Mi'kmaq people have a strong community and culture. We kept playing, having a great time, and it seemed like everyone in the crowd was digging it, too.

Like usual, we were scheduled to play four or five sets that night, and when the first one was done, we came offstage to take a break. I was on my way to the bathroom when Skippy came running out the same door I was headed towards. He grabbed hold of me and started shoving me backwards.

"Get back onstage and do *not* leave," he said. "Someone just got stabbed in there."

A whole bunch of questions started racing through my mind. *What do we do now? Where do we go? Are we going to die?*

It was moments like this where we were reminded just how young we really were, and both of us started shaking in our boots.

One of the bar staff must have noticed us panicking, because he came over. "Don't worry," he told us. "You guys aren't in any danger. Everyone here loves you. It's just one of our regulars. When he gets drinking, this sort of thing sometimes happens . . ."

We couldn't believe how casual this guy was being about someone getting stabbed. But if it wasn't a big deal to the staff, then we decided it shouldn't be a big deal to us, either. The bartender assured us that everything was okay. The guy who'd been stabbed was well enough to walk out on his own, and the guy who'd done it was gone, too. Everyone was so levelheaded about everything that we started to calm down, too. Besides, we had another set to perform.

Just before heading back onstage, Skippy paused and asked, "So . . . do white people ever come in here?"

The bartender looked at him seriously. "No, son," he said. "They aren't welcome."

The comment struck me as a bit odd. As a band full of white kids, the disconnect was jarring, because we were being treated so kindly. But it was his bar and therefore his prerogative, and I realized sadly, he probably felt he needed to have a rule like that because of the way they'd been treated at other bars.

I thought of this incident when, many years later, I discovered a connection in my own family history: specifically, the fact that both of my great-grandmas were Mi'kmaq. It's funny, because as a kid I had lots of friends who were Mi'kmaq, but I never suspected our families were intertwined. I always thought I was Scottish and Irish, and that was it. But some of my uncles did some digging, and now, when I look back at pictures of my great-grandmas, I don't know how I missed it all these years.

Learning the truth about my family history has been an incredible journey of discovery, and it's made me rethink a lot of things about my family and myself. Why do I love hunting and fishing so much? Why do I always want to be outside? Well, because that's how my great-grandparents spent so much of their lives. The more I learn about my Mi'kmaq heritage, the more excited I get. It's like my family tree is one of those paint-by-number drawings, and only now do I have the numbers to make sense of it all. The more we understand our own cultures, the better off future generations are going to be.

Experiences like that stabbing in Saskatoon showed me a lot about the darker side of human nature. But I saw plenty of the good in my fellow humans, too. I once saw a man get down on one knee and ask his girlfriend to marry him in the middle of one of our sets. And it was always such a delight to watch elderly couples get up to dance whenever we played one of our older country songs—these folks weren't dancing to anything else, but as soon as they heard the opening bars of their favourite Buck Owens song, it was time to boogie. I'll always treasure those memories of the power of music to bring people together.

It's what kept us going, too. There were lots of things that could have turned us off being on the road, but no matter how rough it got, the drive to play music always kept us coming back. So did the fans, some of whom remembered our names the next time we came through their town—even though our job as a cover band was to make listeners think about *other* groups. We realized we were starting to make a name for ourselves, and slowly climbing the ladder of success.

After a few years on the road, we had graduated to playing what you might call the AAA circuit. This meant bigger venues—like Saskatoon's Texas T (again, sadly no longer there), which held around 1,500 people—and people paying cover to see us specifically. These crowds weren't just country rock fans. They were fans of *us*. And sometimes they'd even follow us from venue to venue, town to town. What a feeling!

At a certain point we decided we had built up enough of a following that it was time to move to the next stage of our careers and start writing and performing our own songs. It sounded like a good idea at the time, but looking back, I think we were a little premature in that line of thinking. We did start writing our own material, but it was so amateurish and derivative that every time we'd throw an original number into the middle of our sets, the audience would disengage. I couldn't blame them. They didn't want to hear original songs from a band who'd never tried that before. They wanted to hear proven, established hits. Still, it was a hard pill for us to swallow because we wanted to be liked for who *we* were. We wanted to find our own voice—and, one day, a record deal.

Now that I've got a couple of decades' worth of experience under my belt, I can tell you that this process takes a lot longer than you might think. It took me many years to find what I would now call my voice as a performer and songwriter. Because, as funny as it sounds, I didn't really understand what my own voice was supposed to sound like. As a cover singer, it was my job to mimic a bunch of other singers. I would study their music for hours so I could replicate exactly what they sounded like—and yet what we call someone's voice has to do with a lot more than just what is produced by their vocal cords. It's a full-body performance that involves a person's facial expression, the way they breathe, and the way they carry themselves onstage. Take someone like Clint Black, an amazing singer who makes a very particular facial expression when he sings: his eyes squint, his cheeks come up really high, and his lips purse so much his mouth is almost entirely horizontal. To this day, when I sing a Clint Black song, my entire face changes, and I'm instantly brought back to those early days of touring, when other people's songs were all I had.

## Chapter Seven

# JEN

F lin Flon, if you've never been, is one of Canada's great mining towns. It was founded in 1927 by a company called Hudson Bay Mining and Smelting, and the local geology, full of copper and zinc ore, has been called one of the richest mining belts anywhere on earth. In wintertime, Flin Flon reminded me of a TV show I used to watch as a kid called *Space: 1999*. There were several feet of snow on the ground, and the intense moonlight lit up the whole area as far as the eye could see—including the mine, which is still there to this day.

Our first trip to Flin Flon had been in 1991, and a year later the band came back to play there again, this time at a country rock bar called the Unwinder. But on this trip, I wasn't feeling the excitement of our earlier tour because, truthfully, I was in a pretty fragile state.

Just a few months earlier at Christmastime, I had been through some tragedy, and I was holding myself responsible for it. If I'm being honest, I was in a bit of a downward spiral.

Without getting into too many specifics—because this isn't really my story to tell—I had gotten engaged, but we had decided to break it off. Both of us were way too young to be even thinking about marriage. But she had taken the breakup very hard. It was an awful situation, and rather than go to counselling, which is what I *should* have done, I decided I would just put my head down and try to work through it.

For whatever reason, it was in Flin Flon that I finally hit the wall. I had been to the gym earlier that day and was walking back to the hotel in my shorts, as it was unusually warm for spring in Northern Manitoba. The roads were all paved, but off to the sides it was all sharp grey gravel. During my walk, I tripped on something and landed on the gravel with both knees, driving quite a few stones into my skin. It was incredibly painful, and while it was happening, I remember thinking it was almost preferable to the emotional pain I was going through.

I've always been a man of faith, and in that moment, I just started praying. Without getting off my knees, I asked the Lord to please send me somebody. I needed guidance in my life, and I couldn't do it myself anymore. I needed someone who could show me that love was a good thing—that it didn't always end up in disaster and heartbreak. Then I got back to my feet, wiped away the blood, and went back to the hotel. I changed into sneakers and jeans, my favourite AC/DC T-shirt, and a ballcap and headed to the Unwinder to set up for the gig.

As always, it was our job to carry in our gear and set it up ourselves. This process usually took a couple of hours, depending on how hard it was to hang the lights (because, oh yeah, we had to do that ourselves, too). Then our sound tech had to check all the consoles and make sure everything worked properly.

Back then, there was no privacy involved in this process whatsoever. The bar was open for business, and anyone who wanted to could just wander inside and watch the sound check as it was happening. That's different now, thank goodness. These days I much prefer doing sound checks without having the public looking over my shoulder, though I do organize special exceptions for kids with type 1 diabetes and their families. Anyway, this place was full of regulars, who were all having a drink and socializing and doing their usual thing while we tested out our gear and got everything ready for the show that night.

My mind was still on my personal troubles when the front door of the Unwinder opened. You could always tell when the door opened because a flash of daylight would blast its way into the bar, which was otherwise darker than the inside of a cow. But this time was different, because of the woman who opened that door, and who was now walking inside. She was dressed casually, in sweatpants and glasses, and had her hair pulled back in a simple ponytail. But at a single glance, I knew: this was the most beautiful woman I'd ever seen.

I wasn't expecting to have a spiritual experience in the Unwinder, but this was an angels-singing-hallelujah kind of moment—to me, anyway. (To this day, Jen giggles whenever I tell this story, and always says something self-deprecating like, "I have no idea what you saw in me. I looked like hell." But I beg to differ. She never has looked that way, and to my eyes she never will.) When Jen walked into the bar that afternoon, I actually felt my heart start to speed up. This was it. *This* was the person I had asked God to send me. I knew it in my heart as much as I knew that 2 + 2 = 4. It was as if I were hearing God's voice in my ears: *This is who you're supposed to be with. This is what true love looks like.*

Of course, Jen didn't know that, poor girl. In fact, she didn't even notice me when she first walked into the Unwinder. And in a way I'm glad about that, because I could not stop looking at her, and she might not have appreciated this stranger in the corner ogling her without blinking. In fact, I prolonged our sound check for as long as possible, just to stay in the bar and keep an eye on her. The rest of the boys kept saying, "Okay, we're done!" and I said, "Well, let's just run 'Copperhead Road' one more time. I'm not hearing it quite right . . ."

It turned out my intuition was right, because twenty or thirty minutes later, she got back up and headed for the door. I realized she wasn't there for the show, only to visit a couple of her friends. When she left, I felt like a popped balloon. My heart wanted to run after her so badly, but my brain stopped me—thank goodness. What would I have said to her? But then again, what if I never saw her again? What if that was it?

My next thought was: *I've gotta find this girl.*

Now sound check couldn't end fast enough. The rest of the guys went back to the hotel, but I decided to go for a walk around town. I set off on foot, looking everywhere for this mystery woman. Did she work at the restaurant? What about the gas station? When those didn't pan out, I went back to the hotel, jumped in the van, and started driving through downtown. I was peering down every alley, every side street, just in case I caught a glimpse of her. Again, no luck. Eventually I went back to the hotel and sat in my room alone, feeling like I'd totally blown it. But we had a show to do that night—our usual run of four sets of forty-five minutes apiece—so there was nothing to do but get up and get on with it.

I stepped onstage that night and felt myself going through the motions. I was hitting all the right notes, but there wasn't a lot of passion behind it. All of a sudden, I looked out at the dance floor and I couldn't believe my eyes. There, swaying to the music, was the same stunning woman I'd noticed earlier in the day—but now she was also dressed to the absolute nines. Her glasses and sweats were gone, replaced by a stunning outfit and a hairdo with that big '80s tease to it. *Oh my God*. The band was in the middle of a Diamond Rio tune, and I missed an entire line of the lyrics, just because I was so gobsmacked. I had to pretend to cough so that nobody would think anything was wrong.

For the rest of the night, my only goal was to catch her eye. Finally, we ended up making eye contact, and she smiled at me. I swear, it felt like my heart was going to fall out of my chest. This was the feeling I had been praying for.

It wasn't until years later, when we were long since married with kids, that Jen asked me, "You do know I wasn't actually looking at you that night, right?"

"What?" I said.

"I was looking at your drummer, Skippy. He was the hot one, not you!"

When I heard that, I absolutely lost it laughing. And now that I think back to that night, it makes a lot of sense, because I was not the eye candy of the group. In fact, I suspect I was pretty goofy looking. Skippy, on the other hand, had the Bon Jovi hair and the rock-star swagger that drove girls crazy. I couldn't really blame Jen for looking past me.

At the time, though, I was sure it was fate. Once our set was done, I went right over to talk to her. It was almost as if I had no say in the matter—I felt like something, or someone, was pushing me in her direction. It was the strangest feeling, and a big part of me wanted to fight it, because I wasn't the kind of person who struck up conversations with random strangers, let alone the most beautiful woman I'd ever seen. I was shy. I was quiet. And yet I couldn't stop moving, until finally I was standing in front of her and introducing myself.

We started talking. The bar played prerecorded music over the sound system between our sets, and I used that soundtrack as an opportunity to ask her to dance. She agreed, and let me tell you, holding her for that first time was incredible. It was like touching one of those plasma balls from science class—I felt like all the hair on my body was standing up on end.

Sadly, the dance had to end, and I had to get back up on-stage for our next set. For the rest of the night, I just prayed to God that she might want to see me again. Luckily, we were in Flin Flon all week, so I figured I had a chance. I asked Jen afterwards if she would come back and see me again, and she did. That second night, we got to talking a little more, and she told me about her lifelong love of horses, and how one day it was her dream to own her own ranch. When she told me the story of how her grandpa once sold her favourite horse, I could still see the pain on her face, all those years later. I really admired that passion, and how full of life she was in general. By the end of the evening we had agreed to start dating.

It was a bit of a funny arrangement because we both knew I was going to be leaving for the next town come Sunday. But there was no way I was going to walk away from this opportunity that God had basically placed in my lap. How could I?

—

If time isn't linear when you're on the road, then it turns sideways when you're on the road and in love. Depending on what you're doing, a minute can fly by in the blink of an eye, or it can take forever. The latter was the case when I was away from Jen. Those first few weeks back on the road after meeting her were some of the worst of my life. Without her next to me, I suddenly felt empty. I was still dealing with a lot of grief from my past relationship, and I would continue to deal with it for many more years to come. But when Jen was there beside me, making a point of telling me how good of a job she thought I did at a given show, and how much she loved my voice, I knew I could get through anything.

Communication back in the day was a lot trickier than it is now. We didn't have the internet, of course. Hell, I didn't even own a cell phone. So for Jen and me to talk, I would have to call her up on a pay phone to see where she was and what she was up to. It turned out that she didn't actually live in Flin Flon anymore—she had moved to Lethbridge, Alberta, for college, where she was studying travel and tourism, and was only back home for the break between semesters. As we tried to figure out a system for keeping in touch, we struggled with the limits of technology at the time. I remember once saying to her, "Wouldn't it be cool if there was a phone where you could see each other as you talked?" We both laughed at how improbable it sounded, and yet here we are, all these years later, talking over FaceTime when I'm on tour like it's no big deal.

We tried to talk on the phone every night, but sometimes it was hard to find a pay phone. Other times I'd call and she was already asleep. But it was always worth it, just to hear each other's voices. I considered it the best 25 cents I ever spent. On the other hand, nothing was worse than when we'd pull into a new town and I couldn't find a phone in time. It was agony not being able to speak to her, even just for one day. Sometimes, just to make sure we got in our daily phone call, I would pull the van over mid-drive, at some random Husky station, just because I'd spotted a phone booth out front. God love the boys in the band for putting up with me and my love-sick ways.

This method of communication worked out okay in the summer and the fall, but the winter was a different story. That was when I truly came to appreciate the beauty of phone booths, because at least they gave me a bit of shelter from the wind and the cold. But a lot of the time it would just be a phone on a pole, and that was it. Then I'd have to put up with whatever Mother Nature had cooked up for me. I felt like a mail carrier out there, with my sworn duty to fulfil: one way or another, I was going to make that phone call.

For the next two years, Jen and I dated, and, in those tiny windows of time when I *wasn't* on the road, we started building a life together. I moved my stuff from Nova Scotia out west to Alberta, and we even rented a place together outside Calgary. Jen finished her degree and was looking for work. Neither of us had lived with a significant other before, but it was a great arrangement in the short periods we'd been able to be together in person, and I was desperate for more.

Living in the prairies also gave me access to a lifestyle I'd always dreamed about. Jen was a horse girl, through and through, and had grown up riding horses at her grandfather's place in Swan River, Manitoba. (Whereas my only experience with them was the time I snuck up on a Clydesdale at my buddy's grandparents' house back in Nova Scotia.) The horses were out in the field, grazing, and Jen and I'd climbed up on their backs. It was a long way up, though, and we had to bring chairs out with us to give ourselves a boost. Then we just sort of sat there while the horses kept grazing, oblivious. But I felt like a real cowboy, inspired by the John Wayne movies I used to watch with my papa—who actually *had* been a cowboy, back before he lost his farm to the bank and had to go into coal mining. Thanks to Jen, and the southern Alberta prairie, now I was able to do it for real.

Eventually I reached a point where I just couldn't take touring anymore. One night while on the road, all of my anxieties came spilling out of me during our phone call.

"It's too much," I told her.

"But you have to," she said. "It's your job."

She was right. This was the life I had built for myself, and I couldn't walk away for no reason. But when I looked at the rest of our upcoming tour schedule—we had just set out for three or four weeks in a row—all I felt was despair. That's when I decided: *I'm going to ask her to marry me.*

Jen was twenty years old at the time, and I was twenty-three. We were both young. Marriage seemed like a big leap, but I knew in my heart we were meant to be together.

On the night I proposed, I took Jen out for supper to the revolving restaurant located inside the Calgary Tower. Even though the restaurant never stops moving, I can still see in my mind exactly which way we were pointing, and which landmarks were visible out the window in front of us, when I got up from that table and down on one knee. I asked her if she would marry me, and she said yes. Then I placed an embarrassingly tiny engagement ring on her finger—the kind of ring that a musician could only barely afford. But Jen's never been a fan of things like fancy jewellery. To her, a home-made birthday card is the best gift you can give someone. Our love was so strong that she didn't think twice about the size of the rock.

We planned the wedding quickly, because we decided we wanted to get married that summer in Flin Flon. There was a part of me, however, that wondered if it was all a mistake—not my mistake, but rather Jen's. Here I was, sweeping her off her feet at twenty years old, but what if she wasn't ready? Given what had happened in my past, there was a part of me terrified that it was once again too soon, and that I would end up ruining her life. That worry stuck around in the back of my mind for a long time.

Soon the day arrived. June 25, 1994: the greatest day of my life. My mom and dad and sisters flew out from Nova Scotia to be there. So did my aunt and uncle, along with their family. Most of them hadn't met Jen yet, but once they did, they loved her right away—everyone does. It was a big wedding, though of course Jen's side was a lot bigger than mine, being that we were in her hometown. And the ceremony itself was perfect. We got married in the Catholic church in Flin Flon, and as I say onstage, when I play my song "Slow Dance," which I later wrote for Jen, the wedding was one of just a handful of times in my life where I felt my knees actually knock together. The reason I had gone knock-kneed there was anticipation, mixed with fear: I was terrified that Jen wasn't going to show up. Or, worse, that she would walk halfway down the aisle before turning around and running the opposite direction. I'm not exaggerating. These worst-case scenarios were running through my mind on a loop—that the love of my life was going to come to her senses and refuse to marry me after all.

But she did show up, thank God, and when she walked down the aisle, I swear she was the most beautiful bride I'd ever seen in all my life. You can keep every other image of every other bride in magazines, in movies, on TV, whatever. It doesn't matter how much money those other women might have spent on their dresses, or what Photoshop filters worked their magic after the fact. None of those pictures can touch how stunning Jen was on that day in 1994.

The wedding was also when I officially became a member of two different families. Even though I was taking their daughter from them, Jen's family accepted me right away. I owe her parents so much for their unconditional support of our love, especially at that age. My parents were wonderful, too. They never questioned me about being too young for marriage, because they knew that my feelings for Jen were the real deal. As with so many other things in life, it was nothing but support and love.

## Chapter Eight

# ECSTATIC TO BE EXHAUSTED

O nce the marriage was official, and the dust had settled a bit, I became even more resolute in my devotion to Jen. I was never going to leave her side—literally. So I decided to do something I'd been thinking about for a long time: I quit music.

By this point the band had broken up. Touring had taken a toll on all of us, and several of the members were looking to settle down with their own families. That's exactly how it was for me: now was the time to turn my attention to being a husband and, God willing, maybe one day a father. Something my own dad had told me, when I was young, kept ringing in my ears.

"This is how it works," he'd said. "You marry a girl, you have a family together, and you work your tail off to provide for them."

It was a simple philosophy, but it stuck with me. Being a family man meant putting food on the table, paying the bills, and generally *being there* with the people that I loved. The life of a touring musician just didn't fit that pattern. So I sold off all of my electric guitars, plus most of my leftover gear, and went looking for a new career.

But what? That was the million-dollar question. I'd spent so much time laser-focused on music that I wasn't sure what other skills I even had to offer. Well, time to find out! Without much in my bank account to fall back on, I started applying for any job I could think of.

Thanks to my pre-med background, I had a good knowledge of biology, which helped me briefly land a job as a beef inspector at the Canadian Food Inspection Agency at Cargill. Working on what they call the "kill floor" gave me such an appreciation of how careful and humane most beef-processing plants really are—even if the work could get a little gross at times. Whenever I was on duty inspecting organs, for instance, part of my job was to cut into the cows' livers. These livers often had sacs of pus inside them, and if you accidentally sliced into one of the sacs, it was like an explosion. So much pus would shoot out of these sacs that it would hit the other inspector working on the opposite side of the table. I got nailed so many times by those things in my first month there. It was an unusual learning curve, for sure.

Another time I was hired as a bill collector, and got fired a week later because I was so bad at it. I just didn't have the heart to tell these people, "You have to pay or else." I mean, they *knew* they owed money. Why make them feel bad about it? Clearly it wasn't a good fit.

A job I genuinely wanted, however, was police officer, and so I was excited when I got called in for an interview with the Calgary Police. The guy interviewing me wasn't much older than I was, and when he asked what I'd been doing since university, I told him I'd been a musician. But, I added, I'd always loved police work, and had a bit of experience in the military, even though my type 1 diabetes had kept me out of pursuing it further.

He looked me dead in the eye and said, "You don't have any life experience. My advice is to go out and get a real job, work that for a few years, then come back and apply here again."

I was stunned. "I *have* a real job," I said. "I've been a professional touring musician for the last five years."

"No," he said, "that's a hobby. Go get a real job."

I walked out of that interview with my head hanging low, let me tell you. This guy wasn't malicious, either. Unfortunately, a lot of people don't think of music as a real job, and there's not much you can do to convince them otherwise.

By then we were living south of Calgary, in an apartment in the basement of a house on an Arabian horse ranch where Jen had been hired to help out. It was an old place, and there was a lot of moisture in the basement—but it was ours. We were excited to start our new life as a married couple, even though we really didn't have much to our names. At the wedding, we'd been given a bunch of gifts, like coffee makers and toasters, and we needed all of it. But we were so broke in those years that we couldn't even afford coffee filters. Instead, we would use paper towels, because they were cheaper. (This works pretty well, but don't try using the same towel more than once. Trust me, it doesn't end well.) Later in life, we did the math and realized there were several times we were living below the poverty line. But it never occurred to us at the time that we didn't have a lot, because we had each other. And that was enough.

Even without steady employment, I was determined to not let Jen down. I was willing to do whatever it took, but for one reason or another none of these jobs felt like a career. Whereas the one thing I knew I could always fall back on was music. It was the only skill I had that people would pay me to do. Luckily, in my rush to sell my touring gear, I'd held on to an acoustic guitar or two, and I returned to playing music— this time in nearby bars, as opposed to endlessly being on the road. It wasn't much, but it helped. And the best part was I got to sleep in my own bed every night, and I was never away from Jen.

All my semiregular gigs were in a town called Okotoks, typically at a place called Mavericks, where I played weekends for four sets each night. In that sense it wasn't much different from what I'd been doing on the road with the band. Only here, it was more intimate: just me onstage with a guitar. To fill out the sound I also brought along a keyboard, which had a sequencer that I used to manually record and play back individual parts for the missing instruments. It was a neat challenge to have to program drum patterns, for instance, by hand. I used that keyboard to build tracks that I could then sing along with—the usual country repertoire, everything from Clint Black to Garth Brooks, which by that point I was very familiar with. The whole process sounds a little complicated, but it worked out pretty smoothly.

Between Jen's job on the ranch and my gigs, we made ends meet for the next four years. But our lives were about to change. We were renting a double-wide trailer in a trailer park when Jen told me the news I'd been waiting for since the day of our wedding: she was pregnant.

I've always known I wanted to have kids. But whenever I

brought it up, Jen always said, "Not yet. Let's take some more time." I respected her wishes, of course, and tried my best to only bug her about it once a year or so. But when she finally told me the news, that day in 1998, I started crying. It was a feeling of pure joy. At the same time, I had a sense of: *Be careful what you pray for.* After all, was I sure I could really take care of a kid? I could barely dress myself. And what if I wasn't a good parent? Like with many first pregnancies, there were a lot of emotions involved over those nine months.

With a baby on the way, we decided it was time to finally buy our first house together. We had our eye on a house in the town of Okotoks itself, and went to the bank to apply for a mortgage. But they took one look at my job history and said, "Oh, you're a musician? No thanks."

All I can say is thank God for Jen's parents. They co-signed on our mortgage, while I literally wasn't allowed into the meeting. Instead, I stood outside the bank and waited for all the papers to be signed in my absence. Looking back on it, I can't deny that it hurt my pride a little. But most important was that our family was going to be taken care of. I didn't care how it happened. You could call me any name in the book, so long as that mortgage got approved.

Our first home was in an area of town called Woodbend. Okotoks was a lot smaller then—there was literally one traffic light when we arrived—and the people were all so welcoming to us. For instance, there was only one pharmacy in town, and I got to know Mr. King and his wife pretty well over the years during my regular visits to get my insulin refilled. It was such a wonderful community, and Jen and I made some lifelong friends there.

As Jen's pregnancy progressed, she started to feel nervous

about the birth, like any new mom does. As for me? Terrified, as usual. I had always wanted kids, and now that we were starting a family, I had to wrap my head around actually becoming a parent. How would I provide for everyone? What if I wasn't a good enough parent? Was it too late to go back to med school?

In the meantime, we were getting a crash course in the headaches that came with being homeowners. I soon came to regret not paying more attention to my dad, who was a whiz with those small around-the-house jobs, when I was a kid. At least I could still call him up, and he'd answer any questions I had without laughing too much at my inexperience. Slowly, the house started to feel like our home. A big reason for that feeling of comfort was our dog Zeus. He was a big, slobbery Rottweiler who easily weighed over 100 pounds, but a guard dog this was not. Zeus loved everybody he ever set eyes on, and it was hard not to love him right back.

Having a house of our own also had a huge effect on me creatively. When the band broke up, I had hit a wall. Being on the road so relentlessly had killed my creative spirit, because I was spending all my time playing other people's music. It wasn't until I left that I realized I was being stifled in that way. When we moved into the house, I had the idea to set up a little mini-studio downstairs—basically just me, a desk, a chair, and a four-track recorder—and started writing songs again. I was still playing most weekends at Mavericks—and the steady income was a relief, especially with the baby on the way—but those basement sessions were where I started to fall back in love with music as an art form. That's where I wrote songs like "Her Everything," which is all about Jen, obviously, and "Soul of a Horse," which was the first time I tried to capture the feeling of being on horseback in music. At the same time,

I never stopped looking for other work. Even when music was helping pay the bills, I still wasn't confident it was something I could do long-term.

In September 1998, Jen went into labour and I drove us at full speed to High River, where the closest hospital was.

Let's just say the delivery did not go exactly as planned. Our baby wasn't cooperating and the doctor at High River put Jen in an ambulance and sent her off to a specialist at a bigger hospital in Calgary, some forty-five minutes away. When I heard that, my whole world felt like it was about to crumble.

When you're a single guy, life is simple. When you're married, it gets a little more complicated, because now there are two lives you're responsible for. But when there's a third life involved—a life you helped create—it all feels so fragile.

I fell to my knees in the middle of that hospital hallway and prayed. Then I jumped back in my truck and followed the ambulance all the way to Rockyview Hospital, where the specialist was already there waiting for Jen. This specialist was older, and seemed a little bit cocky, but you know what? He probably had the right to be. This guy knew his stuff—and, 31.5 hours of labour later, our son, Kale, finally showed up. There wasn't much time to celebrate, though, because we were all immediately sent back to the hospital in High River, where Jen and Kale stayed for a few more days to recover.

The whole thing was overwhelming, even to an observer like me. There was really nothing comparable to watching the person I loved beyond the word *love* give birth to another person who, it turned out, I loved just as much. In those situations you think to yourself: *How much love does a person have?* An awful lot, it turns out.

Life as the dad of an infant was full of adventure. I learned how to change diapers, and in the process got peed on more times than I can count—and laughed my butt off every time. I also learned how to survive when your usual eight hours of sleep becomes three. You learn a lot about self-sacrifice in situations like that, and how you'd go without sleep for weeks if your child needed you to. (I'm pretty sure Jen did this literally.) I was in awe of how quickly Jen transformed in her new role as a mom. She was so in tune with Kale that she knew he was hungry before he even had a chance to cry. This meant, of course, that I was now second fiddle in her eyes, and I was fine with that. From that moment in Rockyview Hospital forward, it was now the three of us, all growing together as a family.

As it happened, we weren't a trio for very long. Jen and I decided that we wanted our kids to be born close together so that they would be peers and be able to enjoy each other's company as they grew up. Less than eighteen months after Kale was born, Madison came along—poor Jen! But we quickly settled into a routine that was just awesome. We were exhausted, but ecstatic to be exhausted. Our house was full of energy and chaos, and we were still struggling financially, but neither Jen nor I would have had it any other way.

A few months after Madi was born, however, Jen went back to riding horses for work. One day she was invited out to a branding, and I stayed home to look after the kids. I remember I was lying on the floor, playing toy cars with Kale while Madi was napping, when the phone rang.

"Jen's been in an accident," the voice on the other end said. "You have to come to the hospital in High River right away."

When I heard that, my blood froze. I have a really big red button inside of me that has "PANIC" written on it. If it gets pressed, it doesn't un-press. And in that moment, I pressed that button, hard.

I didn't even stay on the phone long enough to get the whole story. Friends of ours came to watch the kids, and I tore off in our old blue truck as fast as that thing would move. I burned so much rubber on that single-lane highway that cars actually pulled over to let me pass. Once I got to the parking lot, I drove straight up to the emergency room doors and jumped out, with no time to even turn the engine off. Inside, I ran around frantically until I found Jen. She was in a bed, conscious, but covered in bandages and restraints so that her neck wouldn't move. Finally I was able to get the rest of the details. It turned out she'd been off riding our horse after the branding when something had spooked him. Jen had been thrown to the ground and broken and compressed multiple vertebrae in her back. The outcome wasn't clear, but she would likely be paralyzed for life.

It was devastating news, and I hit my knees to pray. I knew Jen was strong, but that was when I discovered just how strong. She needed to calm *me* down in that moment, because I was freaking the hell out. I remember she just kept repeating, "It's all right, honey. Everything's going to be all right." But there was a shake in her voice I'd never heard before, as if for the first time she didn't quite believe what she was saying.

Over the next few days, my entire world shifted on its axis. Our friends Tim and Brenda stepped up to look after the kids while I stayed glued to Jen's bedside. Her family, meanwhile, flew out from Manitoba and pitched in with whatever was needed. Unfortunately, that's where we saw firsthand the limits of the Canadian health care system.

Up until that point, we believed, like most Canadians do, that our health care was the best in the world. But Jen's accident made us realize how much improvement our system really needs.

Jen was moved to another hospital in Calgary, where she had access to all kinds of specialists, but the one thing they didn't have was room. Instead, Jen was put in the hallway of the emergency department for two days, and from there was moved inside—I'm not exaggerating—an actual utility closet. That's when something inside me snapped. My wife was in a body brace, unable to move, and was being kept in the same place as the cleaning supplies. That was not how it was supposed to work in Canada. We couldn't treat our sick and injured population this way. But there was nothing we could do.

But then, after three days, we got the news we hadn't even dared to hope for. The neurosurgeon came into the utility closet and said, "We've done all of our tests, and I'm happy to say there's nothing for me to do here. She doesn't even need surgery. She's going to be okay."

Not only was Jen not going to be paralyzed, but she was on track to make a *full* recovery. Neither of us could believe it. She was a walking miracle. And once again, I chalk it up to the power of prayer.

"Thank God," I said, over and over again. And I've never meant it more.

She wasn't out of the woods entirely, of course. There was an intense physio regimen Jen had to go through at the hospital, and when she finally came home, weeks later, she was still in the body brace the hospital had given us. Recovery was a torment for her, because she couldn't even pick up her kids. But she's such a strong lady—way stronger than I am—and she got through it all like a champ.

One day she'd finally had enough, and she said, "There's no way I'm letting some doctor tell me I can't hold my son." I knew it caused her so much pain to put Kale on her lap, but it never showed through her smile.

## Chapter Nine

# SLOW DANCES AND SECOND CHANCES

L ife was finally starting to settle down out west. In the summer of 2000, three months after Jen's accident, I was hired as a protective services officer—also known as a provincial constable—up in what's called the Municipal District of Bonnyville. This is an area in east-central Alberta, next to the Saskatchewan border, that has a population of around 13,000 spread across 6,000 square kilometres. It was so beautiful and serene, and Jen and I were blessed to make a home there.

We found the perfect house on this little acreage that felt like we were in the middle of nowhere. If you think I'm exaggerating, the nearest town was a place called La Corey, and its population was all of fifty-nine. We had no neighbours at all within shouting distance. Our road was a gravel road that hardly any other vehicles used. It was that level of peacefulness.

Kale and Madison loved it there, too, and so did our dogs—particularly our black-and-tan coonhound, Harley. This dog was hilarious. Mostly he'd just lie around, and the kids would as often as not lie right on top of him, which he loved. But whenever we let Harley outside by himself, he would go off and hunt bear—or at least he'd try to. There were a number of bears in the area, and they probably just laughed at him, but he took it seriously. Sometimes Harley would take off into the forest for several days at a time, and we grew worried sick about him. You'd hear the occasional howl in the distance, and that was Harley's signal to us that he was on the scent of a bear, or a cougar, or something else out of his weight class.

The longest Harley was ever gone from the house was four days. When he finally came back, he was skin and bone. This dog had just about run himself to death. Jen took one look at him and went and got a big cattle syringe, filled it with chicken-soup broth, and then squirted it into Harley's mouth, one swallow at a time. Lo and behold, the dog's strength came back. But we didn't let him outside on his own anymore.

Our house was a split-level with cedar shake on the outside and cedar on the inside, and the place smelled like a ski lodge. The entire house was heated by a double-door woodstove located in the family room downstairs, which grew so hot in the wintertime we couldn't sit in there without sweating. Powering that stove required a lot of physical labour. Jen and I would climb into our old 1973 GMC long box truck, and drive into the woods to look for deadfall. Luckily, the forest floor was covered in old fallen trees, and we would cut them all up in manageable pieces, haul those out of the woods and hoist them into the truck bed, and bring them back to our house. Then we'd have to chop the wood again into smaller pieces fit for the stove and cover the piles in tarp so they wouldn't get wet. During one particularly long winter, we ended up going through seven full cords of wood. The kids were too young to help, but in a funny way it was quality time for Jen and me, blisters and all.

Most of my work in Bonnyville was highway patrol. Sometimes that meant going to the scene of an accident, or handling the odd neighbourly dispute, but mostly it was traffic offenses. One of the major benefits of a job like that was that there wasn't any commuting. The Municipal District of Bonnyville takes about two hours to travel from corner to corner, and to save time I worked it out so that I could park my police truck at the house overnight and work all the way home. Then the next morning, as soon as I hit the road, I was on the clock again. It was a great arrangement.

Like with any job, there were downsides, but I like to concentrate on the funny memories. Like one time in December, I was out running radar on one of the highways, where the speed limit was 80 kilometres per hour. I watched this one vehicle approach but couldn't believe the reading on my radar gun: it was nearly double the limit. So I threw on my lights and siren, and pulled the woman over. In this situation the first thing I always asked people was, "Are you okay?" Because sometimes there are emergency situations involved, or people are trying to get to the hospital. You just never know.

"No, I'm fine," the woman said. "I'm just on my way to work. I'm really sorry." Then she paused. "This isn't an excuse, but I'm just going to tell you the truth."

"Okay . . ."

"Christmas carols make me speed," she said.

Apparently, this woman loved Christmas music so much that when a carol came on the radio she started singing along at the top of her lungs and stopped paying attention to anything else.

I started laughing, and so did she. "That's some great spirit you have," I said. "Next time maybe just make sure your foot isn't attached to your vocal cords."

Of course, getting lost in music was something I knew all about. I was still playing gigs when I could, mostly at pubs in the area on the weekends, and had dreams of one day playing in front of much larger crowds. But I also brought along my home studio from our old place in Okotoks—although "studio" might be stretching it a little. Really, it was a tiny little room underneath our staircase, maybe six feet by four feet. I could barely squeeze myself in there with a guitar. But that studio was a special place for me.

I even ended up recording a record there for a buddy of mine. I played the instruments from the room under the staircase, but for his vocal parts I stuck him in the bathroom, which had better acoustics, and where I could run the XLR microphone lines. It was an unusual arrangement, but this guy was a fellow Maritimer who'd also served in the military, so we got along just fine. Another friend of mine, Dean Brody, came up from Edmonton for a couple of weekends to work on some songs together. We ended up writing a couple original songs there, including "Good Day to Ride," which is about the beauty and majesty of the mountains in Alberta, and "Sacrifice," inspired by my granddad's life as a coal miner. These songs in particular really rekindled my love of songwriting, and got me thinking: *Should I record these for real? Could I maybe release them as singles? Would anyone listen?*

While we were finding our way in Bonnyville, the unthinkable happened: September 11, 2001.

That morning, I got up early as usual, kissed everyone goodbye, and was halfway to my truck when Jen came outside and said, "Honey, you have to come back inside—*now*." I thought something must be wrong with the kids and ran back inside without even taking my boots off. On our TV were the images of that infamous day, and we stood there with our mouths on our knees, watching it all unfold. Then I got the call on my radio: all officers had to get to their detachments immediately.

That was the first and only time I left my yard with my lights and siren on, and I drove like that all the way to the detachment. By the end of the day, everything started getting shut down. Not far from us was the military base in Cold Lake, and the whole place was sealed off, with a perimeter established around it. This might sound like an extreme reaction, but you have to remember, at the time nobody had any idea where these attacks were coming from, or who might get targeted next. All we knew was that it was big. Even at our detachment, we set up check stops and generally went into a protective state, making sure everyone in the community was safe.

It was a scary time. We didn't know if anything was coming, but we had to assume that it was, just in case. And then . . . we just sat and waited, not able to do much except be prepared for the worst. That's what we did, not just that day, but for the next few weeks, until life slowly went back to normal. Or so we thought.

We were living in Bonnyville when my dad called me to say that his cancer had returned for a third time. He'd first been diagnosed a couple of years earlier and had gone into remission. But cancer—as a lot of people unfortunately know—tends to come back. And that's what happened with Dad. He'd beaten it twice now, and this time, he told me, things weren't looking good.

As I heard his voice coming distantly through the receiver, it really hit home how far away we were from each other. It was painful to realize I was an entire country away from him, and so were his only grandkids. Jen and I didn't even really debate what we had to do. We both knew it was time to go back home.

I gave my notice at work, we listed our little cedar shake house for sale, and suddenly we were all headed back to Nova Scotia, with no prospects for our future—only faith that the Lord would provide for us.

Dad had always been such a source of support to me throughout my life, and it was time for me to do the same for him. He was always a reserved guy, so I just did my best to give him some quality time—with me and Jen, but also with his grandkids. But he didn't have a lot of energy. One time I dropped by to visit, but before I knew it, he apologized and said he needed to take a nap. It was tough to see.

But it was good to reconnect with my family. Nanny was also there, as were a bunch of aunts and uncles, and we all came together to do everything we could to be there for Dad and support him in his time of need. One silver lining was getting to introduce the whole family to Jen and the kids. That was such a special experience, and we shared a lot of fun times and family suppers together.

At first, we stayed with my parents, but we were going to be there for the foreseeable future and eventually needed to find our own place. That place turned out to be a little

125-year-old farmhouse not far from Mom and Dad's, maybe eight or ten minutes' drive, in a community called Hopewell. It was a great town, beautiful and quaint, and our house was located right by the railroad tracks. That last part might sound nice, but we learned the reality very quickly when the first train went by and the entire house started to shake. The house in general needed work—which wasn't a surprise, given its age. None of the floors were quite level, and the living room was so tilted that we used to joke we should polish the hardwood floor and have baby races on it. The first diaper-clad kid to slide down and reach the other corner of the room wins! We spruced up what we could. We stripped all the paint off, and repainted the whole thing with the help of Jen's parents, who came down from Flin Flon to pitch in. Over time, we made a house a home, as the saying goes.

And our kids got another taste of country life. The house sat on about an acre of land, and our neighbours were a pair of retired farmers, though the man still tapped trees for maple sugar. There was also a farmer who kept cattle in a nearby field, and that's how Madison got her nickname: the Cow Whisperer. Even though she was still quite little, she would stand by the fence and the cows would trot right over to her. Madison could reach out and put her hand on their noses and they wouldn't even flinch. It was really something to see, and gave us an indication that she could have a nice life around animals one day.

Once we'd settled in, that small detail of employment felt a lot more real, but music was still my most reliable skill, so off I went again, picking up gigs at local pubs around Pictou County, earning around $75 each weekend and feeling happy to get it. I played my usual repertoire of country music, but threw in Celtic songs and folk songs, which I'd also grown up listening to, and they were a big hit with the locals. Jen, meanwhile, had a whole series of jobs, teaching kids how to ride horses, cleaning barn stalls, and helping at a vet clinic—sometimes working all three jobs at once so we could keep food on the table and diapers on the babies.

With Jen working three jobs, and my work limited to the weekends, I became Mr. Mom around the house, changing diapers, preparing bottles, doing endless loads of laundry, you name it. At the end of the day, when Jen would come home from work, exhausted, I would be at the front door to meet her, equally exhausted. But it was worth it to spend so much time with the kids when they were that young. I noticed that the more I was the primary parent in the house, the more the kids would come to me when they had a problem or hurt themselves. I drew on those memories, years later, when I wrote "Madi's Song (The Man She Thinks I Am)," which includes the line: "I make her boo-boos go bye-bye." I would never trade that time as Mr. Mom for anything.

And Jen and I always made sure to find some time for us—even if it was just sharing a thirty-second slow dance in the living room before falling asleep. Years later I would use the memories of those evenings together for my song "Slow Dance."

I'd also moved my studio into a bigger room than the last one, though this time it wasn't insulated, and sometimes it got so cold in there that I got used to making music in my winter jacket. Recording music in my little home studio all those years had forced me to figure out one piece of equipment at a time, and by the time I had moved back to Nova Scotia, I was a self-taught engineer, a skill that opened a lot of doors for me.

One day I got to talking to a buddy of mine named Dave Gunning. We'd grown up together, and he was now a recording engineer who, like me, had a studio in his house. When he told me that two other guys in New Glasgow, who ran a music store called H & R Music, were thinking of building a commercial recording studio in town, I jumped at the opportunity to get involved. Together, the four of us found a great location in New Glasgow and built a beautiful facility. Then we opened our doors, and started recording a whole lot of music.

Getting to engineer and produce at that studio was a lot of fun, and we got to work with a ton of fantastic musicians. Unfortunately, it never really made any money, in part because we opened at the exact time when the technology around recording was changing at a rapid clip: from reel-to-reel tapes to digital audiotapes to computers and hard drives, all in the span of a few years. But the work made my heart sing all the same. What's funny is that I actually ended up producing just as many rock albums, and Celtic albums, as I did country records. Not many people know that. But it wasn't like I stamped my name on everything I worked on back then, and I certainly wouldn't have been stamping the name George Canyon—because George Canyon didn't exist yet. I came up with that name later on, when I drove past a street in Calgary called Canyon Meadows Drive and thought, *Hey, that sounds pretty good*.

Meanwhile, my gigs in local pubs were slowly starting to build up steam. I was still playing whatever kind of music the regulars were into, but I found my interests gravitating more and more to just country. I had also written a bunch more original songs by then and was sprinkling them into my sets wherever I could. But now something interesting was happening. When I'd finish playing one of my originals, someone in the audience would me ask what it was called, or who wrote it—and they couldn't hide their surprise when they learned it was me. Then, the next week, they'd show up and ask to hear the song again. That was a great feeling. I'd written songs my whole life, but it was special to hear them go over so well in a live setting.

When I had songs I really liked, I also tried recording them. At first I used my little home studio, but I also worked out deals where local investors would pay my way down to Nashville, or New York City, so I could squeeze in a quick recording session. Once I managed to get some time in a studio owned by Jon Bon Jovi's uncle Tony, and he told me fantastic stories about how Bon Jovi would sneak into that studio after hours to work on his own music. I even managed to get meetings with a couple of record labels, including once with the president of Capitol Records. It was kind of them to give me the time of day, but nothing ever came of these meetings. It wasn't that I was told outright that I wasn't good enough. All they ever said was, "You're not quite what we're looking for," or, "The material isn't strong enough." I didn't take it personally. Over time, I started to understand that *no* really meant *no—for that day*. But tomorrow was a brand-new day. Just because something doesn't click today doesn't mean it won't suddenly click tomorrow. You just never know.

Being back in Nova Scotia was a creative time for me, but I also learned the importance of slowing down. In February 2004, the infamous White Juan storm hit Atlantic Canada, bringing a massive amount of snow and hurricane-strength winds that blew the snow into drifts, some of which were well over my head. Juan dumped so much snow on us that it covered the front door of our farmhouse and the only way we could get out was to climb out of the second-floor window, onto the roof, then down onto the snow. It reminded me of when I was a kid, and my papa would tell me about these legendary snowstorms where the snow went all the way to the tops of the telephone poles. I never really believed him, but we had these shorter rows of poles that ran alongside the train tracks—and lo and behold, the snow from Juan just about covered them entirely. Maybe Papa was right all along.

The storm forced us to enjoy each other's company and our surroundings a little more. Once I'd dug the front door of the house out, we still couldn't drive anywhere. The vehicles were completed buried. So the kids and I decided to build an extensive network of tunnels in our yard. It was a game for their benefit, of course, but I ended up having just as much fun in there as they did. All told, it took the county nearly a week to get all the roads cleared, and in the meantime, we were able to turn a horrific storm into a great family adventure.

While life went on in all these ways, my reason for being in Nova Scotia was still Dad, and it was especially important to me that he got as much time with Kale and Madison as possible. Unfortunately, the cancer got slowly but progressively worse, and he ended up developing tumours in his lungs and his brain. In one of our last conversations, he told me to watch over my mom and my sisters, and to take good care of his grandkids. I promised I would.

Not long afterwards, the doctors decided to treat Dad's tumours with radiation, but it didn't help—in fact, the radiation caused further swelling to the brain, which in the end was a godsend, because it was clear to everyone that Dad had already suffered enough. He went into a coma, and was only fifty-seven years old when he took his last breath. I was sitting with him, in our family living room, next to my mom and both sisters. When it was over, a sense of peace came over the room, but I still walked outside and screamed bloody murder into the night sky. I needed to let out all of the anxiety and emotion that had built up inside of me. I wasn't even screaming words. Just noise.

I miss my dad every day. But at least I know where he's at, and I know I'll see him again one day, good Lord willing.

On the evening Dad passed away, I drove back to Hopewell in a state of shock and grief. What would people say to me when they found out what had happened? What would I say back to them? How could I be there for my mom and sisters? My mind was racing with all these thoughts.

My dad's passing also got me thinking about my own time on this earth and it brought into focus how important it was to enjoy every day—because you never know how much life you have left. Everyone hears stories of people on their deathbeds, with all these regrets about their lives, and I didn't want that to happen to me. When I went home to be with the Lord, I wanted it to be with a smile on my face. I wanted to be grateful for absolutely everything.

For years I'd struggled, emotionally and mentally, to figure out what sort of career I was supposed to have. I had an incredible family, and I never took that for granted. But I was working all these jobs, and none of them felt like a fit. Where did I belong? What was my purpose? Driving home that evening, I realized: *This isn't for me to decide. It's already been decided for me.* Thanks to my faith, I trusted that the Lord's plan was perfect, whereas mine was flawed. I decided then and there to fully relinquish management of my life and my career. Now I was putting my full trust in Him to lead me in the direction I was meant to travel in. Sure enough, it all started to fall into place.

It's funny how the world works. Just a few weeks after I'd made that conscious decision to stop trying to control my future, I got a phone call from an agency in Calgary, who I'd worked with in the past. The agent on the phone said, "There's this TV show called *Nashville Star*, and they're about to hold auditions for season two. We were wondering if you'd be interested in auditioning."

## Chapter Ten

# *NASHVILLE STAR*

The phone call caught me completely by surprise. My first thought was: *How would I even do this?* We weren't exactly flush with cash for random trips to Calgary, where the audition was going to be held. I only made $75 a week, and Jen was already scrambling enough as it was. But it was tempting. In fact, we were already fans of the show and had watched the first season together. When Jen got home that night, I told her about the phone call, and she was adamant that I go.

"If you don't," she said, "you'll regret it for the rest of your life."

Mom agreed, and even loaned me the money for a plane ticket. Then I talked to some friends in Calgary and arranged to stay with them, so I wouldn't have to spring for a hotel. All of a sudden, it seemed possible. So I got on the plane and headed back west, still grieving for Dad but determined to make the most of this opportunity.

The audition was at Ranchman's—a bar I knew well, but

only by reputation—and I met up with some friends for supper ahead of time. As we chatted and laughed over the meal, I began to relax. I decided I was going to just have fun and enjoy this blessing as it was presented to me. If nothing ever came of it, so be it.

For the performance, I'd decided to go with a song that I'd sung onstage countless times before: Johnny Cash's classic "Ring of Fire." I gave it my all, and when I was finished, the crowd applauded and the judges thanked me for coming in.

And—that was it.

The audition was over almost before I knew it. But as I walked off that stage, I could feel the smile on my face.

Back at home, Jen and Mom were both so excited to hear how the audition had gone, and I tried not to get their hopes up. If I'm being totally honest, there was no part of me that believed I actually had a shot of making the show. By that point I'd been in the music business, in one way or another, for more than a decade. I knew all too well how hard it was to catch a break, and how little control the performer has over their fate in the industry. So much of it boils down to luck, and other factors outside of your control. I came to Ranchman's to have a good time, and I'd had one.

But about a week later, the phone rang again. This time it was the producers of *Nashville Star*.

"George," they said, "we really enjoyed your audition. You seemed so relaxed up there, and you had this big smile on your face all the way through, like you were just happy to be playing music."

I told them the story of my dad, and what I'd learned

following his death. Then they invited me down to the second round of auditions, which were being held in Philadelphia.

The first thought I had was: *I'm going to have to hitchhike, because there's no way I'm borrowing more money from Mom for another flight.* Thank God their next line was: "Don't worry, we're covering all of your expenses from here on in." They also said I could bring a player to accompany me onstage.

I knew exactly who I was going to take: Dave Gunning, my childhood friend and partner on the New Glasgow recording studio. He was giddy at the news and agreed right away. In preparation, we ended up rehearsing two songs together: "Ring of Fire" and "Sacrifice," an original song which I'd written with Dean Brody a couple years earlier.

Dave and I then flew down to Philadelphia, where they put us up in a hotel. This time, I found myself getting a little more nervous about the experience. Everything seemed just a little more real. But, again, I vowed to focus on having a good time, and not worrying about anything else. I told myself I was just there with my buddy, and we were going to play a little music together.

The second audition was in a club that was a lot bigger than Ranchman's. But we walked in with our heads held high, and we came away happy with how both songs came off. This time I actually got to talk to the judges, and they were very complimentary, and thanked me for coming all the way down from Nova Scotia. There was no ego involved; it was just a nice conversation. I also got to talk to a few of the other potential contestants, and they all seemed like great people. In all it was another positive experience—and then we flew right back home again, and tried to go about our regular lives while we waited to hear any further news.

The next phone call came a week later. To my utter and complete surprise, they were inviting me to be on the show, along with about twenty other contestants. But, the producers added, the competition would start right away, and by the end of the first episode, only eleven contestants would be left to battle for the title of North America's next country star.

I was so shocked by their offer that some of details, I'll confess, went in one ear and out the other. But the most important facts were crystal clear. I was going to Nashville. I was going to be on TV. And I was going to get to be able to play a song. What more could a guy need?

We had a big celebration at home when I found out I was going to be on the first episode of *Nashville Star*. Jen and I both went into a state of what I can only describe as happy shock. Getting on the show meant that all those years of blood, sweat, and tears—all the times I was away from home, not being there to teach my kids how to ride a bike or tie their shoes—weren't spent in vain. They were worth something. Nothing was guaranteed, of course. But suddenly there was a glimmer of light in a dark room.

There was a fairly long waiting period between my second audition and the beginning of the show, but then the show-business machine kicked into gear. First, there were multiple contracts and other documents to be signed, including nondisclosure agreements and—most exciting to me—a tentative record contract with Sony. The grand prize of the show was a full recording contract, but the rest of us had to sign a shorter document stating that, should we survive past the first episode into the top 11, we agreed to give Sony right of first refusal on any eventual record deal, no matter where we ended up finishing in the show. Signing that clause was a surreal moment for me. After spending so many years chasing my dream, now a record contract—or at least the possibility of one—had landed in my lap.

Preparing to go to Nashville was also a thrill, but I should back up a bit and say that I'd actually been there quite a few times already. Like every other aspiring country music artist, I knew that the United States was home to the biggest record labels, and that Nashville was where the genre lived and breathed. So I'd ended up in the city at various points over the years, trying to get my name out there and collaborate with local musicians. Big Al Downing, for instance, was a great artist who'd once been named *Billboard*'s New Artist of the Year back in the late '70s, and I was blessed to worked on songs with him multiple times.

While I waited around for the first episode to be taped, I went to everyone I could think of in the industry and asked for their advice on how I should prepare for the show. One suggestion I kept hearing was to get out on the road and play some smaller shows as a warm-up and so I connected with some buddies out west, and we booked a little tour together. At this point a few people might have known who I was from my earlier touring, but mostly it was just anonymous work to get in some practice playing with a band. So I borrowed another friend's old SUV and took off through Western Canada in the dead of February.

The shows were a lot of fun, and reminded me of my first tours on the road in the '90s. But this time there was one big difference. Now there was a glimmer of excitement that I'd never really felt before—a feeling that, no matter what, my career was headed somewhere new. *Something* was going to happen as a result of being on this TV show. Sure, it might only be a few good gigs in the immediate aftermath of getting kicked off the first episode. But even that would be a huge step up from where I was.

Once the mini-tour out west was finished, I returned to Nova Scotia, where I kept playing pubs while waiting impatiently for the calendar to move. It was here, at those local shows, that I felt another change in the atmosphere. Now a bunch of people who'd heard the news about the show came up to congratulate me, and they also started requesting my original material more loudly and more often.

Finally, it was time to go to Nashville. The night before I left, I remember having a conversation with Jen.

"I think I'll be okay," I said, "just as long as I don't have to perform first."

I've said this to fans countless times over the years, but I knew that this show was *it* for me. If I pooped the bed on live TV, I would never get another chance like it again.

The good news, however, was that I'd already had a long

career in music. I knew—all too well—how to grow and learn from past experiences and mistakes, and I think that might've given me an advantage. There were some very serious performers among the twenty of us who appeared on that first episode, and I knew the competition would be fierce. But I was less scared of failure, if only because I'd failed so many times before.

My nerves were also calmed by the fact that the feeling around the show was so friendly and welcoming. Our first meetings were held at the historic Grand Ole Opry—not the original building, but the Acuff Theatre, which is where the Opry is mostly held these days. Walking around and meeting everyone all at once, I felt like a hockey player who'd just been traded to a new team. Even though we were about to be competing with one another, we were all in the same boat: nervous and wondering what was going to happen next. I spent a lot of time with Brent Keith, a young guy from Ohio, and a man from Northern Ireland named Mal Rogers, who was really cool. I also hit it off with Lance Miller, who was a real Southern gentleman, in addition to being an incredible singer, and Brad Cotter, who Lance had also become good buddies with. We all had a lot of laughs in that first week.

Another benefit of being on *Nashville Star* was getting to play with their top-notch house band. Even at my first rehearsal, I could tell their talent was off the charts. Incidentally, I got to play with some of those same band members again, years later, as part of my own shows, which was a neat experience. Anytime you get to work with a band of that calibre, it makes you step up your own game—there were no off nights whenever I played with those guys. To use another hockey metaphor, it was like having an all-star goalie behind you. You just don't have to worry about them. From the first time I met those guys, I knew we'd play well together.

The pace of reality TV is so quick. Everything always seemed to be moving at a hundred miles an hour. One morning we were all sitting in the Acuff Theatre, along with a whole pile of producers and crew members, as the main producer—a guy named Dave—went up onstage and gave us the rundown of what to expect. First, he told us about what had occurred on the show to that point, and how many auditions they'd gone through to settle on us. I was impressed with their thoroughness. It also made me realize, once again, how lucky I'd been to sneak through all those stages and wind up sitting there that morning. I still felt like a complete fish out of water—and not just because I was the only Canadian in the room. But at the same time, I was just happy to be there, flopping around on the beach.

Next, Dave ran us through the schedule. We all had our own rehearsal times to keep to in the week leading up to the show. He also told us we had to prepare for a group number, which they called the "all-sing." This was a song that everybody learned, and each of us got to sing a line or two. (Though with twenty of us competing for screen time, I think I might've ended up with half a line.) Before we knew it, it would be showtime, which would be broadcast in front of a live audience, as well as live across the United States and Canada.

Then Dave pulled out a piece of paper and started running

through the order we'd all be performing in. He looked right at me and said, "Leading off the show will be George Canyon."

I'm pretty sure I wet myself, then and there.

But as the days counted down to the first episode, the production team, the crew, the cameraman, the floor director, the stage director, the band—they all did everything they could to prepare us and make us comfortable. As long as we had a little bit of adrenaline on our side, they said, we were going to be just fine. There was still so much we didn't know, though. We had no idea, for instance, who was going to be in the audience, aside from the judges: a record label exec named Tracy Gershon, radio host Billy Greenwood, and the Warren Brothers, a pair of country artists from Tampa.

The night before the taping, I didn't sleep at all. I just tossed and turned in my hotel room bed, then paced the room, then picked up my acoustic guitar and played my song over and over again. Anything to make the time pass.

It was because of that stress that, to this day, I can't remember the first song I played on *Nashville Star*. (I guess I could look it up now, but that would take the fun out of it, wouldn't it?) It's all a blank in my mind. But the funny thing is that the stress I felt had nothing to do with my upcoming performance, and everything to do with having worked for thirteen years at a career that my family had sacrificed so much for—physically, emotionally, economically. I carried all that weight with me. I knew I couldn't screw up. I had to give this performance everything I had.

That didn't mean I was confident, though. Far from it. In fact, I'd still convinced myself that I most definitely *wasn't* going to make it. But the opportunity to be on live TV, airing across North America, was just too big to squander. Even if I got the boot right away, I could still leverage that exposure into booking some live shows, or at least raise my rate at the pubs I played in Nova Scotia. The actual singing of the song was the least of my worries.

The next morning, I went back to the theatre first thing for a full day of production, including sound checks, final rehearsals with the band, wardrobe, makeup, and so on. I also got to spend a bit of time with Buddy Jewell, who won the first season of *Nashville Star* and had stopped by to make a special appearance on the first episode of the new season. Buddy is the salt of the earth, and it was cool to compare some of our favourite old country songs, and to hear about his experiences on the show.

That whole day was a blur, but there are funny little moments that stand out in my mind. I remember standing backstage, just before the show started, and peeking out through the curtain at the sold-out auditorium. Next to me was this huge power panel, and for whatever reason I found myself staring at it like it was the most important thing in the world. I studied each individual fuse, and the label for each piece of lighting, and so on, one by one by one. And in that moment, I was able to remove myself from the equation completely. My nerves disappeared. It was a true moment of peace. But then, just as quickly, I was brought back to reality as a couple of stage managers ran by to help a contestant who had just thrown up. Hey, we all deal with stress in our own way.

I tried to focus on what was happening onstage in the hopes of staying as calm as possible. I looked out again and saw the band members were all smiling and having fun. The set was professional and beautiful. And the show's host, Nancy O'Dell, was fantastic. She was such a natural, and did her best to make everyone feel like we were just playing a song in our local pub.

Then we went live. I stood in the wings as a short video about me played for the crowd, introducing me and where I was from. When it finished, I walked out onstage and played an abridged version of—well, whatever song it was, and that was it. I was done! *Thanks for having me, Nashville. Time to go back home and see my wife and kids.*

Once all twenty of us had performed, it was time to officially move from the preliminary stage to the show itself—and time to cut a bunch of worthy contestants along the way. Whichever eleven contestants were chosen here would get to go on to the *Nashville Star* house, where they'd spend the next nine weeks together. We all walked back onstage, and the judges started doing the typical singing-show elimination thing, where individual contestants are asked to step forward and are then told, in extremely dramatic fashion, if they're safe or if they're going home.

They called my name, and I stepped forward. I could barely make out the words they were saying, but then I heard, "You're safe." I froze. I felt like there had been a mistake, and at any moment someone would come on the loudspeakers to announce that my name had been accidentally put in the wrong pile. But no such announcement came. Finally, it dawned on me: I was staying in Nashville. I was on the show.

———

It took about thirty-six hours for my new reality to sink in. By the time it had, I was already moving into the big, beautiful old home in Nashville that the production team had filled with cameras to film our every move (with the exception, thankfully, of the bedrooms and bathrooms).

For the next nine weeks, our lives became a reality TV show. This format was part and parcel of the success of the show in its early seasons because the viewers got to feel like they were right there in the house with us. Each episode built up to a live performance of a song we had picked from a master list, but we also had challenges to perform during the week, which were designed to test our professionalism and show how we handled pressure, setbacks, and unfamiliar situations.

I had already gotten my first lesson in how great television is made after we taped that first episode. Once we wrapped for the evening, and the audience had gone home, the producers pulled me aside and told me that I had been chosen to perform first for a reason. They felt I was a confident performer who would make a good first impression on viewers at home and show them that we were a group worth their time and attention. It was a huge compliment, and apparently, it worked out. The main producer said my performance had set the bar for the evening, which in turn challenged the other performers to kick things up a notch.

I couldn't help but be flattered, but there was a part of me that was convinced I wasn't really supposed to be there. My personal doubt was part of the reason that first week was emotional. I was rooming with Brent and Lance, and we had a great time together. But I was also lonely, and missing Jen and the kids—this was the longest we'd ever been apart since we'd been married. I couldn't change any of that now, so I tried to just stay grateful, do my job, learn my song, practice with the band, and generally do whatever was asked of me.

In that first week, we went into downtown Nashville, where I was finally fitted out with a real cowboy hat, as well as jeans and a new pair of boots from this cool old shop. Nashville is such a special place, full of history and culture, and I got a chance to explore the Country Music Hall of Fame and Museum, which is fantastic, obviously, but I also loved visiting places like old Civil War sites, where you can feel the history in the walls. I think it's important that, as humans, we know where we came from, and make sure we don't make the same mistakes again. Getting to see that history face-to-face was eye-opening for me.

As part of the show's publicity, we were invited to visit patients at St. Jude's Hospital and to attend a NASCAR race in Bristol, Tennessee, where I hung out with famed football coach Jimmy Johnson and got to stand in the infield of the track. Then a special stage was pulled out onto the track and we performed in front of a crowd of more than 150,000 people. To say that it was all surreal would be a massive understatement.

The other thing that was new to me was dealing with the media. We had scheduled chunks of time to talk to reporters that started at five or six in the morning, to cover the time difference out east, and ran all the way until lunchtime some days. We would just jump from call to call to call to call. I talked to so many local radio stations and talk shows that it makes my throat sore just thinking about it now. Again, my main feeling was disbelief. *Why do you guys*

*want to talk to me? I'm just this little artist from Nova Scotia.*
Though I'll confess my favourite media calls were whenever
I got to talk to stations in Canada, who were cheering me
on from back home.

I never, ever accepted that I had a shot of sticking around
long-term, but somehow, by the grace of God, I survived the
next episode and moved on into the top 10.

From there, the process repeated itself, week after week,
starting with choosing a song from the master list. I tended
to just go with my gut, and pick whichever song jumped
off the page at me. No particular style or tempo, just blind
faith that the Lord was going to guide me to the right decisions. Even when there was competition to play one song
from the master list, we always handled it gracefully. One
week, I had two songs in mind to perform: a Merle Haggard song I already knew by heart, and this really tough
Brooks & Dunn song. I was leaning towards the Merle
Haggard when I learned that one of the other contestants,
a sweet woman with loads of talent, who had a newborn
baby at home, had run into some scheduling issues. She
didn't have time to learn a new song from scratch, but it
turned out she also knew the Haggard song, so to make
things easier I let her have it. Which meant I had to hole
up in my bedroom in the *Nashville Star* house and learn the
Brooks & Dunn song instead.

There are a lot of incredible singers in country music, but
Ronnie Dunn has one of the most unique voices out there.
It's next to impossible to duplicate his voice, or even come
close to doing the licks he's doing. I've already told the story
of driving around in my parents' Ford Tempo as a teenager,

singing along to a Randy Travis cassette and memorizing his vocal tics. Now I was trying to do the same thing all over again, but with a much more challenging singer—and with only four days to get it right. At times it seemed impossible. But in the end, performing a difficult song on the show elevated me in the eyes of the judges, not to mention the viewing audience at home.

When the producers told me this, I laughed and said, "Well, I'm just glad it was something positive, and not: *This kid shouldn't be singing that*."

Looking back on it, that night was a stroke of great fortune for me. Left to my own devices, I would've done the safe Merle Haggard song, and then maybe I wouldn't have had the opportunity to show the audience a side of me they hadn't seen before. I think it also showed the producers, who knew the situation with this other contestant, that I cared.

Every single show, I assumed it was me who was about to get sent packing. But I still got up there and played my songs as best I could. Week after week, I somehow managed to stay alive.

The momentum kept building, and so did the media coverage: now I was doing interviews for TV and satellite radio networks, which would air across multiple stations across the country. When we did live events, we were swarmed by fans of the show, asking for our autographs. That was wild to me. I think most of the autographs I'd signed to that point were for family members.

As the weeks went on, us surviving contestants became closer as well. We started to enjoy the process of the show, rather than just freaking out about who was going to stay, and who was going to leave. We learned to stay cool and try to have a good time.

For me, one of the highlights was the wardrobe department. I told the people working there that I was open to pretty much anything, because you can't trust me to dress myself. I mean, good Lord, some of the clothes I wore back then—I used to wear a bandana tied around my freaking knee, for crying out loud. For a long time, when I was on the road, I didn't even wear a cowboy hat. It wasn't until I met Jen, and learned to ride horses, that I felt I'd earned it, and wasn't just wearing it as a costume. So anytime the wardrobe folks suggested something, I was more than happy to put it on, no questions asked, and as the show progressed, they even made me my own custom shirts, which felt like the height of luxury.

But I was about to get another lesson in the television business, one that played an important role in what happened next.

Since its inception, *Nashville Star* had aired live in Canada and the U.S., which allowed viewers in both countries to vote on which contestants they wanted to remain on the show. But during our season, a new business deal was being worked out by the network, and I was told that the show was no longer going to air live in Canada. This was heartbreaking to hear. Part of what had kept me going all those weeks was knowing that my family, my friends, and my fellow Canadians were following along from back home, and now there was going to be a delay before the latest results came out. I could appreciate this was all above my pay grade, but I'd be lying if I said I wasn't disappointed.

Around the same time, I was called into one of the producers' office with an unusual proposition. "We'd like to talk to you about something," he said. "What if we changed the narrative a little bit? What if we said that even though you've lived in Canada, you're actually from Florida?"

I didn't even take half a breath before responding. "No," I said. "I can't say that. It just isn't true. I'm Canadian, one hundred percent."

I was confused as to why he was even asking me to consider this, but then I realized the producer wasn't trying to be disrespectful to my upbringing. But he knew that if I could present myself as American, then it might help win over more of the voters and improve my chances of staying on the show—especially since Canadian viewers, who presumably made up a large chunk of my supporters, weren't going to able to vote anymore. Clearly, this was something they were worried about, even though it had never once crossed my mind as a problem.

Still, my answer was no. It wasn't that I had anything against Americans. I'd always thought of them as our cousins to the south, and remembered my granddads proudly telling me how they'd fought shoulder to shoulder with American soldiers in combat. I just wasn't willing to compromise who I was for the sake of a few extra votes.

To the producer's credit, he didn't press it. He didn't ask me to sleep on it, or try to revisit the conversation later. He just said, "No problem. Thank you very much."

That first show after the new Canadian broadcasting rules was a big one for me. For the first time, Canadian viewers couldn't vote—or at least they weren't supposed to. I later heard that some of them found a way around the new restrictions, disguising the IP addresses on their computers. Either way, without the same level of support from back home, it was made clear to me that this next show was probably going to be my last.

And so, I sang my song like it was my last. For whatever reason, the entire spectacle brought out my silly side. I was almost giggling onstage, and I couldn't get the grin off my face. I remember the Warren Brothers said to me, "George, you seem especially happy tonight. Were you dipping into the whisky back there?"

I said, "No, guys, I'm just so darn honoured that I got to be on the show." It was like I'd already been eliminated.

But, sure enough, I got picked again! We were never told exactly how many votes we'd each received, but you could always kind of tell where you were based on the drama of the TV elimination process. Well, they made it a heck of a drama that night. But I got by. And, to me, that was proof that maybe the producers were wrong. Maybe being Canadian wasn't a shot against me after all. Maybe people were just voting for me because they liked me, and nationality had nothing to do with it.

Eventually, there were just three of us left competing for the grand prize: Brad Cotter, Matt Lindahl, and me. Matt was a tall fella who wore blue overalls and carried a washboard with him everywhere he went. He struck me as a kind of minimalist, in that he didn't need much from life—he just wanted to make music and make people happy. And Brad was an extremely gifted writer and performer who, like me, loved every kind of country music. For our final performances, we were each going to sing an original song. We'd also gone to a studio ahead of time to record the songs, and whoever won the competition would have their record played live on TV. In the days before the taping, we were pitched a bunch of new originals to choose from, most of which came from Sony songwriters. In addition to performing the originals live, Brad, Matt, and I had been flown back to our hometowns, where we'd recorded smaller live performances in front of all our friends and family. Clips from these performances would be broadcast during the finale as well.

When I landed at the Halifax airport, it was my first time home in nearly two months. I came out of customs and my first thought was, *What is going on?* There were so many people jammed into the airport, it was like five or six international flights had all landed at once. But no: they were all there for *me*. Thankfully, Jen, Kale, and Madi were all there front and centre, and I went straight over to them and gave them a great big hug. Then we all got onto a tour bus for the drive back to Pictou County.

But the madness didn't stop there. There were people parked on the overpass. Others were waving flags and signs with my name on them. When we got to Pictou County, the atmosphere was like those Canada Day parades that had meant so much to me as a kid. People were lined up on the streets, honking their car horns, and cheering from their lawn chairs. Of course, I had a *Nashville Star* crew there with me, who documented the whole thing and aired some of it on TV during the finale. That was an amazing experience that I'll never forget.

We flew back to Nashville for the final show. I was able to bring in a bunch of family and friends to cheer me on from the crowd. Seeing Jen and the kids cheering me on during my final performance was an emotional reminder of all we'd been through to get to this point. There was so much uncertainty, and I knew this was my last chance for the big record deal I'd always dreamed of. I didn't want to screw that up. But at the same time, there was a kind of calm that fell over me. No matter what happened, I knew things were unfolding in exactly the way He needed them to.

I looked over at Matt and Brad and gave them a nod, and thought about all that *we'd* been through, too. Along with Lance, who had been eliminated the previous week, the four of us had become as thick as thieves. We'd hung out together, talking about music and laughing until we cried. When you share that level of stress with someone, it creates a kind of camaraderie that's difficult to describe. Then the judges began to speak.

In my heart, I knew the judges were going to call Brad Cotter as the winner. And I knew I was going to finish in second. In fact, at the final commercial break, I'd turned to Brad and said, "They're going to announce your name, brother. Just you wait." When that prediction came true and Brad was announced as the winner, I went right over and gave him a big hug. Because I'd had an incredible experience, and I knew my career was never going to be the same again.

After the finale had wrapped, and the crowd had gone home, Jen and I went back to the hotel. There was a moment where I lay in bed and wondered, *What would it have felt like to win?* Because finishing second already felt pretty darn good. As I told Jen before we both faded off into sleep, I wasn't sure if I could handle feeling any better than I did in that moment.

## Chapter Eleven

# A FEW GOOD FRIENDS

T he next morning, I woke up with a new sense of uncertainty. I was grateful for everything that had happened on *Nashville Star*, and excited to be back with my family again, but now that the show was over, I had no idea what was going to happen next. I knew there was so much potential in my future. Now was the time to do something with it.

The biggest question mark in my mind was the tentative record deal I'd signed with Sony. This sounded great, but at the time I didn't quite understand the full extent of what I was signing. According to the terms of that contract, if Sony didn't like the music I made for them, they could've shelved me and refused to release it. This happens to a lot of artists—sometimes they're even signed not because the label believes in their work, but because they're *competition* to another act that the label likes better. That sort of thing goes on all the time, unfortunately. So when I put pen to paper on that contract, I was really putting myself at Sony's mercy. Was I going to get a chance to make and release a record? Or was Sony going to shelve me?

This was in 2004, and in many ways the music industry was a lot different than it is now. There was no social media, for one thing, and no streaming services. Back then, artists counted on their label in a big, big way. It was the label that got their music played on the radio—in fact, in the United States, an artist had to be signed to a major label just to be *considered* to be played on the radio.

All these thoughts were running through my head that morning, and I remember Jen having to talk me down, as usual. "Just have faith," she said, "trust the path, try to make smart decisions, and we'll make them together."

Right away, the meetings began. If you've been in this industry for any amount of time, you've no doubt heard stories about Nashville's Music Row—the home of the business of country music, where all the record labels, managers, and publishers have their offices. Thanks to the success of *Nashville Star*, I knew I had the attention of some of these guys, and I was determined not to blow it.

My first big meeting had actually come a few weeks before the show ended. Back when we were down to the final few contestants, I had a meeting with none other than Bob Doyle, a huge figure in the industry who's best known as Garth Brooks's manager, along with another guy named Rory Daigle. I drove my little rental car down to Music Row, parked in front of Bob's office, and took a couple of deep breaths. His nickname was Major Bob, because he was an air force pilot before getting into music, but I decided I would just call him sir.

Bob's office was in this gorgeous converted house that dated back to the Civil War, full of incredibly detailed woodwork and beautiful stained glass windows. I stood in the entranceway for a minute, in awe of everything, until I heard a voice ask me, "Can I help you?"

I turned to see a secretary standing there. I was a bit flustered and went to introduce myself. "Oh, I'm sorry," I said. "My name is George Canyon, and I'm here to see—"

"Oh, hi, George," she said casually. "Congratulations on *Nashville Star*. Bob's in his office. It's just upstairs, down the hall on the left."

Up the stairs I went, still in disbelief that anyone who worked in that house even knew my name. But as nervous as I might have been, Bob turned out to be just the sweetest guy in the world. He was kind and soft-spoken. In that first meeting we discussed the exciting possibility that he and Rory could act as my managers once the show was over.

"Do the best you can," Bob told me about the remaining episodes, "and what will be, will be. If you end up winning, that's great." Then he paused and said something that has stuck with me to this day. "But if you could finish second, that would be perfect."

At the time, all I could think to say was, "Uh . . . I'll try?"

Now, of course, I get what he meant. Bob knew that if you finished first on a show like that, you had to accept the deal that Sony had you sign. There was no debate or discussion about it. But if you came in second, or even third? Now *there* was room to negotiate.

I went back to Bob's office the day after the finale to see exactly how much room. My Sony deal had already been signed, but Bob was very well known and respected within the industry and had done this sort of thing successfully many times in the past. He went right to work on my behalf, took a meeting with the executives at Sony, and—sure enough—negotiated my release. It was only a couple of days later that he told me the good news, and I was so relieved. Their whole structure in offering those contracts was set up to support whoever won the show, and that was Brad Cotter—not me.

Just like that, I was free! Which led to another worrying thought: *Okay . . . what now?*


It looked like I was going to have to stay in Nashville for a while. But no matter what happened, I didn't want to be apart from Jen and the kids any longer. So that same week we planned for them to move down to Nashville, and us to rent a condo together. The kids were still little enough that they could be home-schooled and their lives weren't uprooted too badly. But moving internationally was still a bit of a process, with long lists of things to pack and other difficult questions, like how to get by without our Canadian health care. Once again, Jen was a rock. While I focused on this career we had built together, she took care of everything else. I was so appreciative of all that she was doing. But at the same time, I had tunnel vision. Because if I wasn't taking advantage of this moment in my career, what was it all for?

I knew that this wasn't the life Jen had imagined for herself. But she also knew how badly I wanted this, and she'd seen how it had tormented me back in Canada, day after day and year after year. I'd fought hard to find a way to both provide for my family and sustain my music career, and Jen knew that I was always willing to do whatever I had to make it work. If that meant handing out traffic tickets, or sticking my head halfway inside a cow carcass, then that's what I did. Now I was lucky enough that music was presenting a path forward. We were finally being given fuel for the rocket, and it was time to light the engine.

Once I was a free agent again, Bob and I started taking meetings with other record labels around Music Row. But Bob wouldn't sit down with just anybody. He was picky. It had nothing to do with money, and everything to do with protecting me, as his client. He wanted to make sure that I was making the right decisions and aligning myself with the right people. At the same time, Rory was doing his own legwork, running around every single day on my behalf. I'll always love them both for their dedication to making it all come together.

One day Bob brought me over to Universal, and they said, "We'd love for you to sit down with Universal South Records," which was their label focusing on country music. I was elated, but Bob seemed unsure.

"Well," he said, "who's running that these days?"

"Tim DuBois and Tony Brown."

Bob brightened immediately. "Done," he said with a smile.

When I heard those two names, I got butterflies in my stomach. Tony Brown was a piano player who had produced a ton of great records when he was with MCA in the '80s and '90s, and Tim DuBois was a hit songwriter in addition to being a mogul within the industry. They both had fantastic reputations, and I couldn't wait to meet with them.

As it turned out, Tony was only at the meeting briefly—just enough time for us to say hello and shake hands. So it was really just Tim and I. Right away, I could tell that he was all about the music and the artist. He didn't seem that concerned with how many records I was going to sell. It was all about putting out the best music possible, while also protecting the artist's integrity and respecting who they were. Tim treated artists like people, not tools in a toolbox.

He was also a total Southern gentleman, with the kind of rich accent that you could listen to for the rest of your life. The first thing he ever said to me was, "Well, mister, it sure is nice for you to come over here and meet with us." I just about lost it. Later, once I got to know him a little better, I told him how much I loved his accent and he just laughed. "Well," he said, "I suppose it's better than you *hatin'* it."

Our first meeting went well enough that Bob and Tim met up a couple more times without me. A little while later, I was called back into Bob's office, where Rory was already there waiting. "Universal wants all of us to come over there for the next meeting," Bob said.

That was great news to me, because I was already starting to get a bit antsy. The more time I spent in Nashville, the more I realized that having done well on *Nashville Star*, as powerful a force as it was at the time, was no guarantee that I was going to get on a major label. The fact is there are so many talented people in Nashville, who come there from all around the world, and for a lot of them it just doesn't work out, for whatever reason. Even the most talented musicians in the world still need luck on their side.

When we got to the Universal South offices, they brought us into the boardroom, where it turned out a big group of people was there waiting for us. Tim and Tony were both there, as were a bunch of other people I'd never met before, from A&R, marketing, and who knew what other departments within the label.

Tim did the talking, and he got straight to the point. "Well, mister," he said, "I reckon we'd like to offer you a record deal."

I was so stunned I didn't know what to say. I think I just stood there for a few seconds. Then Tim started to laugh and reached out to shake my hand.

"Well, yeah!" I said finally. "That would be awesome!" My next thought was: *I can't wait to get home and tell Jen.* This was what we'd all been working so hard for, and now it was finally here.

During all those early years I spent working my tail off, touring the country for no money and playing in whatever bar would take me, I always told myself it was for a purpose—that one day I would get signed to a major record label. That was my be-all, end-all goal. But for some stupid reason (and I'm sure countless other artists have thought the same thing) I always assumed that once I got my deal, everything would become easy. Less stress, less work. It would all just *flow*.

Boy howdy, was I wrong. In a way, signing the deal is the easy part. Once you're on a major label—well, that's when the work really begins.

We started putting together my debut record immediately. The label knew we had a limited time to really take advantage of what had happened on *Nashville Star* and get a record out while people still remembered who I was. There wasn't enough time to schedule a ton of writing sessions with top songwriters and come up with a bunch of hit songs. Tim told me not to worry, however, and said, "We're going to find you the best songs we can. We're going to get you A drawer songs."

I thought, *Wait, what on earth does that mean? Are there actually songs in a drawer somewhere?*

When Tim saw my confusion, he laughed and explained that *A drawer* is their term for the very best songs, followed by B drawer, C drawer, and so on. Generally, the A drawer songs were the ones that only got pitched to artists on a major label. And not even all major-label artists—just the ones who the label felt could take the song and make it a hit. See what I mean? Even after you're signed, you still have to fight for the songs you really want.

So Tim and Tony went to work, and they found me some fantastic songs. "I'll Never Do Better than You," for instance, sounded like a perfect two-step George Strait song. When Tim and Tony first played it for me, we were all bowled over at how beautiful it was. I always try to picture Jen as the subject of a song like that, and right away I could see it. There were other times, however, when I would like a song that Tim and Tony didn't, and then I had to really make my case. One in particular was "Who Would You Be," written by Wade Kirby and Bryant Simpson, which, to me, was perfect. I felt it encapsulated so much of who I was as a person, and a father, and a husband. Tim and Tony weren't so sure, but they respected me enough to go along with my decision. That was one of the reasons I was so glad to sign

My dad, Fred, holding me
as a baby in our single-wide
trailer in rural Nova Scotia.

Here are two of the matriarchs of my family. On the left is Nanny Lays, who everyone called
Honey, and on the right is Nanny Westerman, who was known as Eve to her friends, but to
me they were both Nanny.

I was so obsessed with the air force that I wore this pretend air force shirt almost every day. In this 1978 class photo, you can just see the wing insignia on the left side of my shirt.

Playing for the Westville Miners in 1980. Back then, I thought someday I might make it to the NHL, but God had other plans.

In Aberdeen Hospital in 1984 after being diagnosed with type 1 diabetes. On my shoulder is Gizmo from the movie *Gremlins*.

This blurry photo is of my very first band, Reaction, an '80s-rock cover band. I'm on the far right with the cool lightning bolt guitar strap. From left to right: Linda on bass; Bobby on drums; and Cecil, the lead singer. Not pictured are Karen and Laura on the keys.

With my dad, mom, and two sisters in 1986. Mylissa is on the left and Cynthia is on the right.

When Counterpoint signed with our manager, Doc Holiday, the local paper featured the news. From left to right: Todd Chisholm, or Skippy, our drummer; me; Darren Theriault, our bass player; and Paul Lowe, our guitar player. These guys were more than just bandmates, they were my friends. Sadly, we lost Todd in an avalanche in 2016. A good friend, gone too soon.

Meeting Jen was the best day of my life. In the picture on the left, we are twenty and twenty-three years old. On the right is a photo of us on our wedding day, June 25, 1994.

Me having an early morning cuddle with Kale and Madison in our home in Bonnyville before heading out to do some highway patrol.

Performing in front of friends, family, and fellow Nova Scotians at Glasgow Square in New Glasgow for the *Nashville Star* hometown visit in April 2004 was a surreal experience. (Bruce Murray/VisionFire)

I wouldn't have been able to do *Nashville Star* without the support of my family. In the image on the right, Jen is next to my mother, Cheryl, with Madi and Kale in front at the hometown show. Below, I'm with Madi and Kale walking through the crowds. (Bruce Murray/VisionFire)

In 2008, I went to Kandahar with the band and crew to perform a Canada Day show in support of the troops. From left to right: our security officer; guitarist Erick Hedrick; me; fiddler Shane Guse, known as Goose; Chris Coote; drummer Adam Dowling; keyboardist Mike Little; and bassist Joe Butcher.

Here I am signing the bomb shelter we ran to when, right before our performance, the base was rocketed. After an hour, we got the all-clear and returned to the stage to play the full show for all the troops… and told the Taliban to "kiss our ass."

Accepting the Queen Elizabeth II Diamond Jubilee Medal from my good friend and then–minister of national defence, Peter MacKay, on April 13, 2013, in New Glasgow. In 2011, I had been appointed the first-ever colonel commandant for the Royal Canadian Air Cadets.

In the studio recording my album *Better Be Home Soon* with Richard Marx and the crew in 2010. Richard and I are seated in front.

Rocking out with my band at the Calgary Stampede in 2012. From left to right: Jay Buettner on the guitar, Mike Little on the keys, Ed Ringwald on the steel guitar, me, Adam Dowling on the drums, and Goose on the fiddle. Directly behind me is Chris Bryne. (Neville Palmer Photographer)

*Above:* So blessed to get to tour multiple times with one of my heroes, Alan Jackson.

*Below:* At the 2016 Canadian Country Music Awards in London, Ontario, with country music stars Terri Clark and Gord Bamford. My friend Brett Kissel won Male Artist of the Year that night.

*Above:* In 2014, I became the anthem singer for the Calgary Flames. This was taken on my first night singing in the Saddledome.

*Below:* In 2015, I was honoured to be inducted into the Nova Scotia Country Music Hall of Fame. Here I am performing at the prelude to the ceremony.

Rocking out with Brett Kissel at the Norfolk County Fair in Simcoe, Ontario, in 2015. It's crazy to think he opened for me when he was fourteen years old at the Canadian Finals Rodeo in Edmonton—now look at him. (Jenni Field)

With my brother, Dave Gunning.

Casey Clarke, me, and my manager, Jim Cressman, at Casey's radio show on New Country 100.7 in Penticton, BC, in 2018. Outside of the business, these are two of my dearest friends; I've known Casey twenty years and Jim twenty-five.

With my longtime tour manager and dear friend, Rick Bazuin, at a special performance at Holt Renfrew in 2016. (Rick is also the true star of my music video for "Betty's Buns.")

*Above:* Speaking to kids with diabetes at an aircraft hangar in 2017 as part of my work with "The Sky's Not the Limit" and the Juvenile Diabetes Research Foundation.

*Below:* Flying the RV-7A, one of my favourite airplanes, in military snowbird colours, in 2018. On the side of the plane is written H. Col George "The Chin" Canyon; Chris Coute gave me my call sign, The Chin.

Receiving the Platinum Award for my debut album, *One Good Friend*, in Pictou, Nova Scotia, in 2018 was incredible, and I was with the most incredible people. From left to right: Jay, Rick, Karen Corbin Hughes, Kale, me, Adam, Mike Little, Mike Lent, and Louis O'Reilly from management. In the image below (from left to right): my manager, Jim Cressman; Madi; Jen; and me. (Len Cheverie)

Out for a ride on my first horse, Chester, with our two labs, Rein and Rope, on the High River ranch. (Neville Palmer Photographer)

Fly-fishing down at the famous Bow River, just outside of Calgary. I'm constantly drawn to the water and the land.

My beautiful family in Antigonish, Nova Scotia, in 2018.

If you're trying to find me, I'm on the ranch. (Neville Palmer Photographer)

with them—and another reason to be grateful to Bob for being so picky about who I took meetings with in the first place.

Another time, Tim came over to me and said, "Mister, I got this song, and I caught it on the way to Tim McGraw. Tim never even got to hear it, 'cause I took it! It was supposed to go to George Strait, too, and I told them, 'Don't you dare! It's going to Little George instead!'" (George Strait, of course, is the king of country music, and Tim gave me that nickname as an affectionate way of telling us apart. I took it as a huge compliment to be even mentioned in the same sentence as him.)

Then Tim played me the song. It was written by Rivers Rutherford, who's written a ton of number-one records for people like Brooks & Dunn, Kenny Chesney, and Brad Paisley. This song was called "One Good Friend," and it became the title track of the record. I didn't even have to hear the whole song to know I was going to use it. Once again, it seemed like a song that had been written with Jen in mind. Every word of it hit home.

I said, "Tim, you've got to let me record this."

He just smiled and said, "Why do you think I wouldn't let them play it for anyone else?"

So that's my one little claim to fame: the time I was able to steal a song from Tim McGraw and George Strait. Those guys probably didn't even know it existed, and truth be told, given their success, I doubt they'd care they missed out. But it became a big hit for me. At this point I've released more than thirty singles in my career, and obviously you can't play all of them in a given night. But "One Good Friend" always comes to the top of the list. There are very few shows where I don't play it.

I did, however, get to write with a few people, and those were such fantastic experiences. The songwriters in Nashville are relentless, writing song after song, sometimes multiple sessions per day. It was everything I could do just to keep up with them. To this day, I can't come close to writing at the speed that these guys do. Don't get me wrong: when I'm inspired to write a song, I do it. Sometimes, if I'm really lucky, I can stay inspired for a whole week. But for the pros, writing songs is their job, and they show up and give it their all, every single day.

The most important song that I helped write has to be "My Name." I hate to say it, because I'm very blessed for every song I've ever been pitched and every song I've ever recorded, but some songs in an artist's career just mean more than others. "My Name" is one of those career-making songs for me—and not just because I cowrote it. That song has such truth in it. It's not fiction. It's real.

A dear friend of mine and his wife decided to have kids, and asked Jen and me what it was like. I told him, "There's nothing like it in the world. No matter what you do, nothing will ever compare to being a dad." When she got pregnant, we were all so excited for them. But five months in, she had a miscarriage, and it was just heartbreaking. "My Name" came out of that heartbreak.

I remember the night I wrote the song. Interestingly enough, I wrote it with a fellow Nova Scotian, a guy named Gordie Sampson, who I knew a little bit and who everyone told me I had to write with. He was working out of one of the houses on Music Row, and the two of us were sitting in the living room, trying to think of something to write about. I mentioned this couple from back home, and it turned out Gordie knew them, too, and had also heard about their tragedy. I pulled out my guitar, started strumming a few chords, and the song just started flowing out of me. The melody, the rhythm, everything. It was stormy that night in Nashville, and we could hear the rain beating down on the roof and the thunder crashing, and the whole room would light up every few seconds when the lightning struck. Gordie is one of the best writers Nashville has to offer, and it didn't take him long before he jumped right in, tweaking some of the lyrics, and soon enough we were going back and forth with one another.

At one point he stopped what he was doing, and said, "George, are you sure you want to finish this song?"

I asked him why, and he said, "Well, radio might tear you a new one over something like this. They might not accept it. This one is really, really personal."

"To me, this is what music is all about," I replied. "If I try to build my career only on what I know radio is going to accept, then I'm not being true to myself."

We finished the song that night, and the rest is history. "My Name" is still my highest-charting single. It went number 1 in Canada and number 44 in the States, and it turned out to speak not just to me, but to a whole lot of other people as well. Over the years I've received thousands of emails about this song and what it means. I've also been fortunate to play it live at many functions, including in front of five thousand couples at a city park in Detroit, as a benefit for an organization that supports couples who've had miscarriages. It was a meaningful song, and it also paved a road for me. It signalled to country music fans everywhere that this was the kind of music they could expect from me. I wasn't just trying to chase radio's tail. I was trying to say something important.

Once we had the songs ready, it was time to record them. I remember walking into the studio on the first day of recording and meeting these incredible session musicians Tim and Tony had brought in to play on it. It's funny, because some of them, like the drummer, Eddie Bayers, would wind up playing on a few of my records over the years. Eddie has played on literally hundreds of gold and platinum records and was recently inducted into the Country Music Hall of Fame.

At that point, thirteen years into my career, I'd been in a studio before, but never quite like this. This was the big leagues. I think Tony could tell I was nervous, so to loosen me up a bit he started telling me these wild stories about his career as a piano player. I've always been a huge Elvis fan, and he just about knocked my socks off when he told me that he once played piano in Elvis's band.

"We had this gig in a big church," Tony said. "The band was all set up, and all of a sudden, out comes Elvis." As everyone knows, Elvis had this aura and energy about him, and whenever he walked into a room, people were in awe— including Tony, who was just a young man at the time. The front row of the crowd was full of excited young women, and one of them yelled out, "Elvis, you're the king!"

When he heard this, Elvis stopped in his tracks and said to

her, "No, Jesus Christ is king." Then he spun on his heels and did his signature pointing move—right at Tony, who was sitting at the piano—and said, "Hit it!" The only problem, Tony told me, was that he had no idea what song he was supposed to play.

At this point in the story, I was already in tears I was laughing so hard, and I said, "So what did you do?"

"I don't know!" Tony said. "I just started playing chords!"

We both had another good laugh, and sure enough, for a moment I forgot I was even in the studio.

One thing people might not know about recording is that the musicians aren't all playing in a room together. Usually the singer has to go into a separate vocal booth. Picture a little room inside a larger room, with windows so the singer can see into the control room, where the producer and engineer are working. Back in the day, the control room was where the tape machines were located, but by the time we were recording, everything was done digitally.

When I stood in the vocal booth, I also had a view of the rest of the band—the drummer, the guitar player, and the bass player—who were all recording their parts together. In the business, we call this going "live off the floor." These days, especially during COVID, it's become more common for musicians to record their own parts individually, often in studios that are thousands of kilometres away from one another. This is a cheaper way of doing things, but to me there's still something so special about playing music live off the floor. It creates a kind of magic that you just can't duplicate.

I would sing along with these early takes, but at that point my vocals were what we call scratch tracks, which means they were just rough demos that I would go back in and sing properly once the band's parts were all locked in. But I was still terrified, because I noticed the band members weren't using traditional chords or sheet music. Instead, they were all using this special Nashville number system. So, for instance, if the key of the song was G and we were playing a 1-4-5, that meant G was the one, C was the four, and D was the five. It makes sense if you're used to them, but if you aren't, it can be overwhelming.

We started off with "I'll Never Do Better Than You," and I was looking at this chart in front of me, with these numbers on it, thinking, *I'm lost*. I couldn't even tell which part of the chart was the verse, and which was the chorus. I mean, making this record was a quick process. I knew these new songs, but I didn't know them *that* well. Only two of them I'd had a hand in writing, and the others I'd had to learn in a hurry. Well, I messed that first song up so many times, but the band was gracious with me, as were Tim and Tony. Eventually I started to settle in, and I suppose we must've done a pretty good job, because "I'll Never Do Better Than You" ended up being the first single off the record.

Another highlight from those sessions was recording "My Name," which I remember the band members all telling me had really touched their hearts. There was also "Letting Go," a song I wrote about soldiers who have to take someone's life in combat. That song featured a wonderful vocal guest appearance from Paul Brandt, who is an incredible inspiration and who I'm now proud to call a friend. We'd never worked together before, but when he sent over his vocal part, I got goose bumps.

Before I knew it, the recording was done. And on September 28, 2004, my debut album, *One Good Friend*, was released into the world.

## Chapter Twelve

# WHY NOT?

N ow that the record was done, it was time to take it on the road. In fact, there was a bit of synergy there, because part of the *Nashville Star* deal was that the four finalists would all go on a group tour together. The tour bus came and picked us up right in front of the Grand Ole Opry, and it was a tight squeeze. Normally, a tour bus can hold twelve people, but our group had fourteen. That meant that two unlucky people had to sleep on the couches in the back lounge. We were jam-packed in there, but I couldn't deny it was a cost-effective way of doing business.

The tour lasted about four months, and it took us across America, as well as—thanks in part to my insistence—to a casino in Ontario for our lone Canadian date. Everywhere we went, the reception was incredible. As the only Canadian artist on the bill, I wasn't sure how I would be received, but people in the States have always been so kind to me whenever I play there.

One of the hardest things for me was not to fanboy out

at every turn. Not only was I on an honest-to-goodness tour bus, but we'd pull in to the venue right next to Alan Jackson's tour bus (or one of them, at any rate). We were sharing the stage with my lifelong idols, and I could not wipe the smile off my face. When I got to introduce myself to Tim McGraw, or George Strait, in the green room before the shows, I was so starstruck I'm not sure I was even speaking English.

Still, four months is a long time, and I learned a lot about the business of music in that time: about tour management, accounting, and production, among other things. Lance, Matt, Brad, and I had already become like brothers, so being around one another was easy. But that level of touring put constant pressure on us, and I quickly figured out why some artists turn to alcohol to deal with it. I saw it happen in front of me. One of the positive things about being a type 1 diabetic is that I really can't drink very much. My stomach just can't take it. But there were others around me who I saw lean on alcohol— hard—just to calm themselves down and give them some relief from the stress and expectations.

There were occasional breaks in our schedule, where I got to go back to Nashville for a day or two. But it was tough. Kale and Madison were getting older, and Jen was raising them on her own whenever I was on the road. And even when I was in town, I was still being pulled in different directions for work, taking meetings and sitting in on writing sessions to keep generating new material and moving my career forward. I worked on so many songs that will never see the light of day. Now, I look back on those years and I'm so appreciative at how forgiving Madi and Kale were towards their dad. I missed a lot of stuff, but we did the best we could.

Eventually, though, it became too much for them. It was

the height of summer in Nashville, and the heat was intense. Our condo complex had a pool, thankfully, so the kids could use that. But they really didn't have much of a life in the city.

One day Jen said to me, "Honey, I just don't think this is working."

We talked it over, and eventually decided that it was best for the three of them to move back to Alberta while I stayed in Nashville with the plan that I would eventually join them when I could.

My career was taking off, and there were more and more business details to work out. I got my first business manager through a Nashville company called O'Neil Hagaman, and they did a great job managing my finances. Meanwhile, Bob and Rory worked alongside them, figuring out logistics like when we needed to hire musicians for touring, and how my various streams of income were going to be taxed. Being a Canadian working in the U.S., my tax situation was a little more complicated than usual, but they helped me keep everything straight. We also met with a lot of different agencies that were all trying to sign me. Eventually I chose CAA, who were also based out of Nashville, and they started booking me for festivals and fairs across the country.

This was exciting, obviously, but I also became aware of a new level of pressure on my shoulders. This was the first time where I wasn't just one member of a band—I was the solo artist, and I had to make all the decisions. Now it wasn't just my family counting on me, but also my band members, and in turn their spouses and kids.

I got another lesson in the business of music as I played more around the United States. There was so much competition for live country music that we realized we were actually losing money. Our show wasn't cheap to put on, considering we had to carry all the band members, plus transportation— sometimes we took a bus, but other times we had to fly, depending on how far away the gig was.

After some long consideration, I decided that I had to regroup. Just because my management and label were in Nashville, that didn't necessarily mean *I* had to be there, too. Jen and the kids were already back in Alberta, and I decided to go be with them and pursue my career from back home in Canada.

For her entire life, Jen's dream was to live on a ranch and look after horses. She'd had to put that dream on hold for me to live mine, but now it was her turn. She found us this beautiful piece of land west of High River, not far from where we'd lived before, with a little log cabin and a barn and 148 acres for the horses to run.

While she was arranging to move the kids out to the ranch, I had to break the news to my management that I was leaving Nashville. But they supported my decision and agreed there was really no reason I had to live in town when I was always just a short flight away. So I packed all of our remaining stuff up in a five-ton U-Haul and hit the road out of Tennessee first thing in the morning.

I was so desperate to get back home that I vowed not to stop unless I absolutely had to. I drank a steady supply of coffee, and soon enough it was nighttime and I still hadn't stopped once. I kept going, with the help of some long conversations between me and my Lord and saviour to stay alert—some people call it praying, I call it talking the Lord's ears off. Before I knew it, the sun was coming back up again on a brand-new day. I made it to the ranch, threw the U-Haul into park, and then slept for an entire day once I got inside. I can't exactly recommend this method of travel for others, but it was proof of how stubborn I was, and how desperately I wanted to be with Jen and the kids.

Being at the ranch was like being home again, and it was obvious how happy it made Jen to be there. I hadn't really considered how much she'd sacrificed for me to that point. I feel badly about that. But like my granddad always said: "You can't cry over spilled milk, but you can damn sure get down on your knees and lick it up." The only thing to do now was help her start living her dream as fully as possible. That meant learning all kinds of new chores, such as fixing fences, which took me some time to get used to. (Barbed wire and I still don't get along to this day.) I was also in charge of shovelling out the barns, which isn't a pleasant task at the best of times and is even less so during a −40°C cold snap. But it was satisfying work, especially because I could see how content Jen was.

Truth be told, we all loved being back in nature. Madison loved being around horses just as much as her mom did, and our little 900-square-foot log cabin felt like I was living inside *Little House on the Prairie*, which was one of my favourite TV shows as a kid.

I was also able to recalibrate my career a little and focus on the Canadian market. At first CAA kept booking my shows, but it was a little tougher for them to do so as an American company, and eventually we decided to part ways. Bob and Rory stayed on as my managers, and I signed with Jim Cressman to be my new agent. I've been buddies with Jim for twenty-five years now, and we're really close. Plus, coming back and playing shows in Canada was extra special to me. It was amazing to stand onstage at places like the Canadian Finals Rodeo and hear fans singing my own songs back to me. These were cities and towns I'd been to countless times over the years, but now I had somehow become the act people were coming to see. Everything had come full circle.

Touring could still be difficult, of course. I remember one stretch that involved fifty-two shows in a row, which was intense. But I never felt as far away from home as I had before and seeing so much of this great country of ours helped inspire me to write new music that reflected my surroundings.

My life was starting to feel balanced at last. I'd travel across Canada playing country music, then come home to live and work with my family on our ranch. Finally, it felt like my two worlds were starting to collide.

There was just one thing still missing.


Throughout all the twists and turns my life had taken me on, I never fully gave up my dream of flying. My obsession with airplanes dated back to when I was a little kid, and it was so deeply rooted inside me that I couldn't let it go. I truly feel there's a similar dream inside everyone's heart. Maybe you already know what it is, or maybe you haven't quite found it yet. But if you look deep enough inside yourself, I think you'll see it. Whenever I talk to elderly folks, I'm always amazed at how they all knew what their dream was—and how the ones who never followed it came to regret it.

Now, I wouldn't describe myself as a rebel. Not exactly. But at the same time, I've always been someone who questioned things. So when I was first told I'd never fly airplanes, that was my question: *Why not?*

"Well, because you're a diabetic," was always the answer. *So?*

None of it made any sense to me, and I never accepted it as a final answer. I may have put that dream to one side while I pursued music, but I knew there was no way my Lord and saviour would dangle that kind of carrot in front of my nose just to tease me. I would never do that to my son. So why would He do it to me?

Ever since I was a kid, whenever I looked at a piece of land, the first thing I would imagine is what it would look like with a runway on it. That's how much flying and landing planes is on my mind. So it was only a matter of time until I looked out over our ranch and started daydreaming about it again. *What would our runway look like? And is there a way it could be me up in the sky? Is there something I hadn't thought of yet?* That's when it came to me: paragliding.

If you aren't familiar with it, paragliding is an activity where you put on a harness, including a big fabric wing that looks like a parachute. Then you run and jump off a cliff and let the wing—and the wind—carry you down to the ground.

I decided to give it a try, so I went and signed up for a course in Cochrane, just outside Calgary, which has a big hill perfect for practicing. Unfortunately, on the day we were supposed to do our practical, which is where you actually put all the gear on and fly, I was called away for a last-minute gig and never got to do it. But I still had my paragliding wing. So I decided to teach myself. I looked up a tutorial on YouTube to see how to put the equipment on, and then I stood out in one of our fields and waited for the wind to pick up. A few seconds later, I felt my feet leave the ground.

I wasn't very high up—maybe six inches—but it brought me right back to when I was six years old, leaping off the top of our little hill in Pictou County for a taste of flight. That was the same feeling I had in my paragliding wing. My heart soared, and I knew: *This is what I've been searching for.*

But I couldn't stop there. Again, why would God tempt me with something like this if I wasn't supposed to experience it fully? So I decided to push further. I called up Transport Canada and asked them what my options were. As a type 1 diabetic, they told me I would have to pass a medical exam, but if I did that, I could get something called a recreational pilot permit. This wasn't a full pilot's license, but it let me fly ultralight aircraft, which are smaller propeller planes that hold no more than two people.

Well, now I was really thinking. I remember sitting on a tour bus headed to Edmonton and calling Jen to tell her what I'd learned. "Honey, I've got an opportunity," I told her, "and I feel like I have to take it." She supported me, once again, so I went off and signed up for ground school.

I'll never forget the day I soloed for the first time. My instructor was a guy named Clark, and he was a great teacher. When I got into the ultralight on my own, I thought to myself, *This is incredible! This is awesome!* But when I taxied the aircraft out to the runway and got lined up for takeoff, my thoughts changed to: *Oh dear. Clark's really not here this time, is he?* I took a deep breath, said my prayers, and slowly pushed the throttle up. The plane started moving forward, and when I got to rotation speed and pulled back a little bit on the stick, it popped right off the runway. I was about fifty feet off the ground before I remembered that I was going to have to land this thing all by myself.

The plane kept climbing, first to 500 feet and then to 1,000 feet. Once my nerves started to wear off, I just started giggling, I was so happy. That giggling continued through the entire circuit, all the way up to my approach for landing. And on the way back down, I greased it—which is what we call a perfect landing. As I told Jen afterwards, "If you were up there with me, honey, you wouldn't have even spilled your wine."

When I got back to Clark, he was so excited for me. I had a five-gallon pail of water dumped on my head, which is part of the old tradition for a pilot's first solo, and we took a photo together. It was just the coolest day ever.

From there, I got my advanced ultralight certification, which meant I was able to bring a passenger up with me. Jen refused to come up with me, because she was worried that if something happened to us, there would be nobody left to raise our kids. I had to respect that. Instead I invited other buddies of mine to start coming up with me, and we always had a blast together.

The logical next step was getting my full private pilot's license—but that's exactly what I didn't qualify for, as a type 1 diabetic. Yet the more experience I got flying, the less sense it made to me that this was where I had to stop. Why this plane, but not that one? I wasn't a health risk in any way. I was on an insulin pump and taking great care of myself. It seemed like such an arbitrary line to draw.

I got to talking to a couple of friends of mine within the aviation industry, and eventually I reached out to Peter MacKay, who I'd grown up with in Nova Scotia (he was from New Glasgow, back in Pictou County) and had gone on to be a cabinet minister in the federal government. He told me I needed to meet with the transportation minister and helped me organize a meeting. I flew to Ottawa and made my case to the minister in person, showing him everything I knew about the science of diabetes, including how blood sugar worked and all the tools that diabetics have to keep themselves regulated. From there I was referred to Transport Canada and then Civil Aviation Medicine, where I was asked to be part of a group that was being put together to study issues like mine. We had four different meetings in Ottawa and our conversations were very productive.

At around the same time, I met a gentleman named Stephen Steele, who was a former Air Canada pilot who'd developed type 1 diabetes in the 1980s and was told he had to give up his license. Steve reluctantly agreed, but he didn't drop the issue. He went and got his law degree, then used what he'd learned to fight Transport Canada's rules about being deemed "non-medically certifiable" to fly—and he won! He got his commercial license back in 2001, more than fifteen years after it had been taken from him.

When I talked to Steve, I realized his case may be a useful precedent for what I wanted. Together we took a few more meetings with Transport Canada and ended up spending more than two years lobbying the government to make this change that we both felt was overdue. It wasn't a simple process, and at one point it looked like the rule wasn't going to get changed after all, but finally Transport Canada called me one day and said, "We're doing it. It's done."

Just like that, I could get my full license. And it wasn't just me. There were five of us, across the country, who immediately qualified. What a wonderful day that was.

By that point, my obsession with flying was as strong as it had ever been. I'd gotten my hands on a little old aircraft called a Piper Super Cub, built in 1952 but completely restored. And I even managed to convince Jen to let me put in a runway on the ranch—another dream come true—without taking too much of the land away from our horses and cattle. It was about 1,200 feet long, all told, and the kids helped me maintain it by walking end to end and clearing it of rocks. Once that runway was complete, I could fly my Super Cub anytime I liked.

With the Transport Canada rules changed, I went off right away to get my medical done, complete another round of ground school, and then straight into flight training. Cheering me on all the way was a dear friend of mine named Chris Coote, a pilot who flies for Porter Airlines and who was always giving me advice. He was instrumental in my getting my full license, and was never afraid to motivate me in his own way—I believe his exact words, when I first told him I was trying paragliding, were: "You're going to kill yourself, moron. Get your pilot's license."

I was trained for my private pilot's license by another dear friend named Alex Bahlsen. Alex was a stickler for thinking of every possible situation that might come up when you're in the cockpit. He always said to me, "It's not about *if* you have an emergency in the cockpit. It's about *when*."

I always used to laugh at that, until the first day I had an emergency in the cockpit. One day I took off in an advanced ultralight from High River, and smoke immediately filled the cockpit. I was able to do a 500-foot emergency circuit and cut back in real tight, opening my door in the process enough to clear out some of the smoke so I could at least see through the windscreen. I managed to land the aircraft and immediately shut everything down, right in the middle of the runway. When I opened the doors fully, smoke just started pouring out everywhere. Funnily enough, the airplane itself was fine. The culprit was a single smouldering wire attached to a 12-volt adapter in a GPS unit.

But thanks to my training with Alex, I hadn't panicked. Sadly, Alex passed away a couple of years ago in an airplane crash.

Now that I have my full private license, I carry a bit more swagger when I go for a rip—just kidding. The license doesn't make the pilot. The training does. The education does. And the experience does. I've never gotten sick of it and would fly every single day if I could. Seeing things from the air really changes your perspective. It shows you the beauty and the majesty of all that He created. In my corner of the country, I'm lucky enough to fly past mountains, and foothills, and a gorgeous river. When I get to a stretch where there are no houses and no people around, I can also fly down low along the deck and soak it all in, past eagles' nests and all kinds of other natural wonders. It's a spiritual experience for me, and always will be.

In 2006, for my album *Somebody Wrote Love*, I recorded an incredible song called "I Want You to Live," about a woman whose husband is suddenly killed. The song was written by Michael Dulaney and Robin Welty, and when I first heard it, the first thing that came to my mind was the military. Earlier that year I had the opportunity to fly to Afghanistan, just after the Kandahar airfield was liberated, and I was immediately struck by the incredible bravery of our troops. Some of these men and women were still teenagers, standing in the middle of the desert with an automatic weapon and fighting an enemy they often couldn't even *see*. At the same time, I was also thinking about the family members of those enlisted, who are equally courageous, but who are often forgotten in these discussions of heroism and bravery. I wanted to pay homage to all of the emotion that these spouses, parents, and children go through every single day.

We shot a music video for the song with Warren Sonoda, who's one of the best music video directors in the country, at CFB Trenton in Ontario, alongside some of the troops stationed there. It was an honour to be able to include actual military heroes in the video. Unfortunately, one of the young soldiers who was in the video ended up giving his life not long afterwards in combat in Afghanistan. That tragedy makes the video even more poignant to me now—in fact, I haven't been able to bring myself to watch it since that young man passed. I only wish I could have done more.

One day in 2007, I got another phone call from Peter MacKay. By this point he was the federal defence minister, and he was calling to tell me about the government's honorary colonel program. This was put into place at the end of the Second World War, as a means of helping returning soldiers reacclimate to life in Canada. The program was still going strong to the present day, and Peter asked if I might be interested in becoming one of them.

I didn't need any time to think about it. "Of course I'll do it," I told him. But I wasn't sure exactly what *honorary* meant. "How involved can I be?"

"As much as you like," he said. I could go full on, wearing the uniforms and following all the protocols, or I could take a more casual approach, the way someone like the longtime hockey commentator Don Cherry had, which was more about just being there to help when needed. But there was no doubt in my mind. I wanted to do as much as I could.

During our next phone call, Peter told me he'd spoken to General Rick Hillier, chief of the Defence Staff, and they'd whittled it down to a few remaining candidates—including me. They liked that I'd spent time in the air cadets, and that I had a passion for the military generally. The fact that I had a worldwide career was also helpful, since our troops, of course, are also based all around the globe. Finally they made up their minds, and the job was mine.

Now, an honorary colonel is always attached to one particular place, so of course my next question was: *Where?*

"We'd like you to serve at CFB Greenwood."

Talk about full circle. Greenwood was the same place I'd done basic training as a kid, so it had a special place in my heart. I enthusiastically accepted the position, and before I knew it, I was back in Ottawa getting sworn in. Then it was off to Greenwood, where I met with the wing commander and the wing chief, both of whom welcomed me with open arms. It was such an incredible experience. I used to joke that I jumped straight from corporal to colonel, but at least they both started with a C.

The normal season for an honorary colonel is three years, but the government had the option of extending that term by one more year, so I got to serve at Greenwood from 2008 to 2011. In that time, I got to be an RO, or reviewing officer, for certain squadrons of air cadets at the end of the year—including 374 Squadron in Stellarton, which I myself had briefly been a member of, all those years before. Acting as their RO was one of the proudest moments of my life, and I showed up in full uniform, with boots every bit as shiny as they were when I was twelve.

Volunteering for military events was important to me because I wanted to understand what our troops were really going through. That's why I agreed to get slung out of a Cormorant helicopter, dangling a couple of hundred feet off the ground. It's also why I signed up to travel to Afghanistan along with some of the troops, which once again showed me just how brave and compassionate they really are. I'm so proud of the Canadian military, and I really can't say enough great things about the people who serve their country by being part of it.

I thought that once I'd served my four years as honorary colonel, that would be it for me. But Pete came to me again and let me know that General Hillier had asked if I'd be interested in a brand-new position: the first-ever colonel commandant of the Royal Canadian Air Cadets. They'd had one for army cadets and sea cadets in the past, but never for air cadets. "We think you'd be great for it," he said.

I was deeply honoured. But what they didn't tell me is that to take the job, I had to become an actual reservist colonel. During the ceremony in Ottawa, the navy man who swore me in gave me this funny look, as if to say: *You realize now we could technically send you into combat, right?*

Reading his expression, I just grinned and said, "Put me to work if you want, sir. I'll do whatever you ask of me." And I've been lucky enough to hold that position ever since.

I know I've been blessed to be able to follow an awful lot of my dreams. Do I deserve any of it? No. But by His grace, He's let me do it. That's the blessing of each day.

## Chapter Thirteen

# A SERVANT'S HEART

All throughout my life, I've tried to be someone who serves his fellow humans. There's never a shortage of opportunities, either: when you have that need to serve, you can always look around and find people to help. It has nothing to do with ego, or wanting to shout to everyone around you, "Hey, look what I've done!" It's just an innate drive. Now that I was at a point in my life where I had a little more time on my hands—no longer scrambling to provide for my young family, or busting my hump trying to keep my career alive in Nashville—I was able to apply myself to service with a new level of commitment and joy.

That was a big part of the reason I wanted to be in the military. Even from a young age, I just knew I wanted to serve my country. Years later, when I got into law enforcement, it came from the same place. And now, as a musician, the need to serve was still as strong as ever, and I needed to do whatever I could to see it through.

A lot of this could be traced back to my faith. I was born

and raised Roman Catholic, where I was a reader in church, went to Sunday School, and even taught Sunday School to other kids while I was still young. But when people asked me what religion I was, I always told them, "I'm a Christian. I follow what Jesus said, which is: 'I don't come for religion, I come for mercy.'" God gave me my drive to serve, and my belief in my Lord and saviour was a large part of who I was. But I didn't dictate my life by belonging to one particular denomination. Born and raised Catholic, yes. But ultimately my faith was bigger than that.

That faith took a totally unexpected turn when, in 2014, I became pastor of Living Grace Church, a new place of worship in Okotoks that was open to people of all beliefs and all walks of life. When the church first opened its doors, someone asked me if being a pastor was something I'd always wanted to do, and I had to be honest with them. "I'd never even given it a thought before," I said. "But if this is what God has put in my heart, then okay." I was going to do whatever He needed me to do, because look at all that He's done for me.

The new church may have sounded like a big undertaking, but to me, faith isn't rocket science. It's also not about the four walls of the building, or even about a group of people, as lovely as it is to come together to worship as a group. Faith is about having a one-on-one relationship with God. I've been blessed to have that for as long as I can remember, and this was my chance to try to foster that same relationship in others.

There are plenty of lines in the Bible—which I like to call "the manual," because that's what it is to me, a manual for getting home—about God's love for everybody, and I drew on them all the time during my nine months as pastor. I got to talk to so many people who had been shunned by other churches in the past. One woman told me she'd been having homosexual thoughts, and when she told her previous church, they asked her to leave. She was despondent and felt so alone she was even considering suicide. That sort of thing just broke my heart to hear. I thanked her for having the courage to share her story with me and told her that her relationship with God was between her and God, and nobody else. Who were we, as humans, to decide who God loved? It was like telling a parent they were allowed to love their son, but not their daughter. It didn't make any sense. She and I hugged, and then she continued on her journey. I hope she's doing well today.

I believe that we have to get back to what I've called commonsense Christianity, which, at the base of it all, is about God's love for all of us. We need to do our best to love each other. I know it's harder than it sounds, and trust me, I fail at it every day. But I'm still working hard to understand His words and live by them.

Now, being a servant doesn't always mean starting a brand-new church. It can be the smallest things. If you see somebody drop something, you go out of your way to pick it up and give it back to them. For that one brief moment, you're serving them. You're taking time out of your schedule, and stepping outside of your bubble, and doing something for another person.

For me, one of my biggest opportunities to serve came from an unlikely place: being a type 1 diabetic. When I was fourteen, there were no public figures in my world who had the same disease I did. I had no role models, and no examples to live by. When I was diagnosed, there was a part of me that knew right away—if I ever had a platform, I would use it to help others like me.

So when I got the opportunity to speak to diabetic kids from across Canada and the United States, telling my story and hopefully inspiring others to not give up on their dreams, I didn't hesitate to take it. I started arranging for special meet-and-greets with kids with type 1 diabetes before and after my live shows, and I gave keynote addresses all across North America for a great organization called Children with Diabetes. I also got to serve as national spokesman for the Juvenile Diabetes Research Foundation, where Dave Prowten and his whole team are doing such amazing work. The work was incredibly satisfying, and it also came with some pretty fantastic perks. Once I got to travel down to Disneyworld along with a big group of type 1 diabetic kids, and Jen and our kids got to come along, too.

One thing I kept hearing from the kids I spoke to was that an awful lot of them had the same desire to fly planes that I did. I think it probably has to do with being told that they can't. Kids generally don't like to take no for an answer, and kids with type 1 diabetes are the most positively stubborn people I've ever met. Their drive, focus, and dedication to their health are humbling. Then you have people like Sébastien Sasseville, who became the first Canadian with type 1 diabetes to climb Mount Everest back in 2008. What an incredible accomplishment that is.

In 2016 I created "The Sky's Not the Limit," a program that was designed to show teenagers that if they learned to control their diabetes, they could still live out their dreams. We chose to focus on teenagers specifically because they can sometimes be the hardest people to convince. At the same time, I've found that if they have a clear goal to work towards, they can be incredibly motivated. Sometimes that involves creating a series of smaller goals along the way. So if, say, you want to make your high school football team, first you're going to need to be in good physical shape, and before you can do that, you need to be totally in control of your blood sugars. Even if the goal seems so far away—like flying a plane one day—they will work hard to try to achieve it.

As part of the program, I flew my little airplane from airport to airport, across the country, to meet with these kids and their families. A group of them would wait in the hangar, and I would taxi up in my airplane, then get out, shake their hands, speak to them from a podium for a bit, and then pull out my guitar to play some songs. It wasn't so much what I said as what they *saw*: I wanted the kids to see me in my full flight suit, so that their dreams would in turn seem a little bit more within their grasp. I travelled that way from the west coast all the way to a tiny airport in Trenton, Nova Scotia, another part of Pictou County.

Some of the stories I've heard over the years have really stuck with me. Once I met a pair of eleven-year-old twins who'd been diagnosed as type 1 diabetics when they were four. But their parents told me they kept forgetting to take their insulin. Well, you can BS a lot of people with that sort of thing, but you can't BS another type 1 diabetic. I knew all the tricks, and this was one of them. So I talked to them for a bit, and eventually got the real explanation. It turned out their teacher had told them they could never become schoolteachers if they were type 1 diabetics—and that was *their* dream, suddenly being taken away from them.

In that moment, I wanted to find that teacher and give them a piece of my mind. But that wouldn't have done any good. The level of ignorance that exists around type 1 diabetes isn't malicious. People just don't know. So I explained to these twins that their teacher was wrong. They absolutely could become schoolteachers if they wanted to. But I encouraged them to also try to teach their teacher—to explain to them what type 1 diabetes really is, and to take that negative experience and turn it into something positive. The more you explain to people what this disease really is, the more they will understand. By the end of our chat, the twins were so excited. I don't know what happened after that, but I'm sure they went back to their teacher and had a good conversation about it.

Another little boy I met was being teased at school—his classmates said the only reason he was a diabetic was because he wanted attention. If he just took better care of himself, they said, he wouldn't be diabetic in the first place. Of course, these kids were wrong, and were referring to type *2* diabetes, which is very different. But that boy's experience inspired me to stand up on my soapbox and use my voice to yell to the highest heavens about what being a type 1 diabetic is really all about.

The fact is, as type 1 diabetics get older, we face additional complications and have to rely more on the health care system than your average Canadian. But if we can be in control of our disease right out of the gate, and stay that way throughout our lives, the system would save billions of dollars—not to mention our quality of life would be greatly improved. We could easily have insulin, insulin pumps, continuous glucose monitors, and testing equipment provided to all type 1 diabetic kids from the moment they're first diagnosed. Without these, scary things can happen. There are so many stories of people having to ration their insulin because they couldn't afford it and getting sick or even dying as a result. (You may remember I even rationed it myself when I was eighteen, and first out on the road with the band.) Insulin isn't covered under Canadian pharmacare, so if you don't have a separate benefits program through your job, you have to pay for it out of pocket. Meanwhile, the price of insulin continues to go up and up.

Some people might respond to that by pointing out there are aids and systems in place, such as a $600-per-year rebate for insulin. Let me put that number in perspective. Personally, I need four or five vials of insulin every month, and each vial currently costs $42. That adds up to more than $2,000 per year. So $600 is a nice gesture, but it doesn't go very far. If people don't have enough money to cover the difference, they will have to do things like rationing the insulin they do have. To me, it's common sense. I believe the government should either provide these supplies for free to type 1 diabetics or give us all access to free pharmacare.

If we all put our heads together, I'm confident we can make this disease a thing of the past, and sooner than people might think. Researchers like Dr. James Shapiro in Edmonton are as close to a cure as anyone has ever gotten. This research is so important, and whenever I hear that the obstacle is money, it really upsets me. Because type 1 diabetes changes people's lives, and the lives of their entire families as well. Dr. Shapiro's work is world-class, and if money is the only obstacle, then that's not an excuse at all.

———

The thing about serving the Lord is that He doesn't see borders. Nor does He see different cultures. Wherever I'm needed, I serve. That's why I've been blessed to also get to travel internationally to help out those in need.

Jen and I have worked with Samaritan's Purse, a Christian aid organization, where we flew to Cambodia and Vietnam to help install water-filtration systems and generate fresh running water for families that had never had it before. Aside from my time in Afghanistan, this was the single most eye-opening experience of my life. When we landed in Cambodia, the first thing I noticed was the smell. It turned out the city's septic system just ran openly down the street. In that moment, I really understood how fortunate we were to live in a country like Canada. But it was when we moved out to the jungle that our perspectives really changed.

The Cambodian jungle was like nothing I'd ever seen before. It was hot and humid, but also gorgeous. As we approached the village we would be working in, we came up to this field, and our guide said, "Do not, under any circumstance, walk off of this path." It wasn't until we entered the field that we saw thousands of little flags sticking out of the ground—each one representing an active land mine, still left over from the Vietnam War. We made sure to stay to the dead centre of that path the whole way, but once we got to the village, Jen and I were shocked to see the local kids running around and playing in the fields, right by the flags! Oh my gosh. Our inner parents came out in that moment, and we started to panic, but for these kids it was a normal situation and they weren't all that bothered by the potential danger.

What really stuck with me, however, was how these folks lived. A family of four would all live inside a hut on stilts, with no doors or windows anywhere, and maybe a pig or two tied up to one of the stilts below. It was a simple life, but I've got to tell you, the people looked so happy. The look they all had was one of true contentment, and it gave me a lot to think about in my own life, where we're all so focused on accumulating more and more.

We all gathered in the main part of the village, and together we mixed up cement and got these filtration systems in the ground. It was a group effort, but the funny thing was that almost no words were spoken, because of course there were language barriers and our two groups couldn't understand one another. That is, until we realized one of the villagers owned a guitar, and I was asked, through our interpreter, if I would play everyone a song.

Hands down, this was the most unusual gig I've ever played. We were surrounded on all sides by the Cambodian jungle, and if you had looked in at the scene from a distance, you wouldn't have been able to tell what decade it was. Of all the songs I knew, I decided to sing "Folsom Prison Blues," by Johnny Cash. And the reception I got from those villagers really touched me. They couldn't understand any of the lyrics, and I doubt they even knew who Johnny Cash was. But none of that mattered—by the end of the song they were clapping and cheering just like any other audience back in North America. Music touches souls, no matter the language.

We had a similar experience in our trip to Ecuador through World Vision, helping get children sponsored to provide them with food, shelter, education, and other supplies. This time Jen and I were able to bring our kids along with us, and it was the first time they really got to see poverty up close. But I'm not sure *poverty* is the right word for it. When I hear *poverty*, I think of sadness. And these people weren't sad at all. They didn't have much in their lives, but they were grateful for everything they did have—including each other. Madi and Kale still talk about that trip to this day, and I can only hope that they grow up with the same servant's heart that their dad has been blessed with.

## Chapter Fourteen

# POLITICS

Growing up, politics was never really something I considered for myself. I always figured the extent of my political career would be the time I ran for grad class president in 1988. Representing my fellow students at West Pictou District High was fun, but I never imagined it would lead anywhere else.

It wasn't until 2006, when I first travelled to Afghanistan, that my thinking started to change. I flew over with Peter MacKay, who at that time was the minister of foreign affairs for the federal government. The flight from Canada to Afghanistan takes a full twenty-four hours, and there's not a whole lot to do. So Peter and I had some long conversations where we talked about everything, but mostly politics. He told me all of these fascinating things I knew nothing about: not just how the system was designed to work, but also the way things so often tended to go sideways.

Peter knew how important it was for me to serve others, and at one point he said, "You know, George, if you ever want to serve your country in the best way you can, you should step up and run for government."

The idea of representing my friends, my neighbours, and my community was appealing. I liked the idea of being a voice for people who don't always get to have one. Peter said running for office was one of the hardest things a person could do, but also one of the most satisfying.

At the time, though, I still brushed him off. "Sure, Pete, that'd be great," I said. "One day I might do that. Who knows?"

Then, several years later, I was asked out of the blue if I was interested in stepping up and running for the Conservative Party. There was a federal byelection in the nearby riding of Macleod in 2014, and they were looking for nominations for candidates. But just as I was considering throwing my hat into the ring, my buddy John Barlow called me on the phone and told me that *he* was planning to run in the same riding. I sat down that night and prayed about what I should do. In the end, I felt I didn't have the right to get in John's way, so I withdrew my name before it ever made it onto the ballots. I could feel I was being called to serve, but not in this capacity.

Flash forward to the summer of 2019. Jen and I were out working in the garden together when I got another phone call from Peter, who told me the Conservative Party wanted to talk to me about the upcoming federal election. At that point, I knew all the candidates were pretty much decided, and I wasn't sure what role I could play. When I spoke to a representative from the party, they wanted to know if I would possibly be willing to put my name in the hat, in case something unexpected came up.

Obviously, I was interested, and flattered that they would

even think of me. It was another opportunity to serve, and it came on the advice of Peter, who was someone I trusted.

Our family then headed up to Flin Flon to stay with Jen's family for a week, and it wasn't until the drive back home that I got another phone call from the party. This time they said something totally unexpected.

"Okay," they said, "it turns out the candidate in your home riding"—not in southern Alberta, mind you, where I'd lived for many years, but rather the one back home in Nova Scotia—"has to step down for personal reasons. We don't have time for a new nomination process. So we'd like to know if we can appoint you for the position instead."

Now, I may not have lived in Pictou County anymore, but I did—and still do—spend about a quarter of the year there. Plenty of my family lived in the area, from my mom to my aunts and uncles to my cousins. Between visiting them, and doing my various charity gigs, I was in Nova Scotia at least a couple of months every year. So it did make some sense that they were asking me to fill in there. Once you're a Nova Scotian, you're a Nova Scotian always.

"That sounds exciting," I said. "Let me talk to my family and I'll get back to you."

"Okay. You have twenty-four hours to decide."

I couldn't believe what I was hearing. This was a huge life decision that would affect not just me but my entire family—and I had *one day* to make up my mind? There were so many factors to consider. Would we have to sell our ranch and move back east? And what if I won? What would that even look like? This was not a simple question, and whenever I do anything, I need to take time to make sure my heart and soul are both on board with the decision.

The drive from Flin Flon back to our ranch took about fourteen hours, and our family spent the entire second half of the trip talking the proposal over. The more we discussed it, the more excited I got about the opportunity. In the back of my mind, I kept hearing Peter's voice from the flight to Afghanistan: *If you want to serve, this is the best way to do it.*

I decided I would do it.

The next morning, I called the guy at the party back. "My family and I have talked about it," I said, "and we've decided that I'm going to do it. What's the next step?"

"We need you on a flight to Halifax tonight," he said, "and you can come down to the riding from there."

I'd barely gotten in the door from our last trip and now I had to leave again. But I threw some clothes into a suitcase, not even knowing how long I was going to be gone for, and I went straight back out the door, this time to the airport. I was excited. But had I known then what I know now, I don't think I would have even gotten on the plane.

When I arrived, I was still totally naïve to how politics works. I'd always assumed that people did things for the right reasons. I assumed that politicians put others ahead of themselves as best they could. I might disagree with them over a given issue, but that's what democracy is all about, right? You're given a platform to serve, and you use it to do the right thing. Well, what I witnessed during this campaign was not the right thing.

I got a bad feeling immediately. When I got to my first meeting with the electoral district association, which is the board that oversees the constituency for the party, there was a strange atmosphere in the room. It had to do with the way some people on the EDA were looking at me—almost as if they were looking down their noses at me. I thought, *Hold on, I've just put my entire life on hold to help turn Central Nova back to blue. So why do I feel like I'm supposed to go to the corner and bury my head in the sand?*

The EDA told me that they first needed to meet with some of the other people in charge, including Peter, and would call me in once they were ready. I assumed this was because they hadn't had time to do the normal nomination process. But at the same time, I was already starting to hear talk that I was what they call a "parachute candidate."

Hearing that sort of thing drove me nuts. It wasn't like I was being dropped into a place where I didn't know anyone and nobody knew me. Nova Scotia was where I was born and raised. My family was here. The only reason I'd left in the first place was because I couldn't make enough money playing music to sustain myself. On top of that, I'd even moved back for a time when my dad was sick. My son went to the same elementary school I had. I was still very much connected to the place. Just because I didn't sleep in Pictou County every night didn't mean I didn't care about the community. It all just felt weird.

In Alberta, I had also been told that the previous candidate had stepped down at the last minute for personal reasons, but once in Nova Scotia, I began to hear from other people that maybe this official story about the end of his candidacy wasn't the truth. That didn't sit right with me.

I'm not a person who puts much stock in rumours. If I want to find something out, I'll go straight to the source. It just so happened that I knew the candidate. He was one of the people who my dad, in his capacity as a marksman, had helped getting their rifles sighted before hunting season, and he would come by the house all the time when I was a little kid. So I called the guy up and asked if we could meet in person.

We ended up sitting in the gazebo in his backyard and had a heart-to-heart conversation that lasted more than two hours. What he told me made me feel nauseated, and embarrassed, and sad. It turned out he never wanted to step down. He was encouraged to by the party because they didn't think he was a viable candidate to win the election (an idea I completely disagree with, by the way).

I was stunned. Just a few days earlier, I had been told that this man had stepped down of his own accord, and that the party needed me so badly because they had nobody else to replace him with. Now it became clear that the reason I was chosen was because the party felt I had a better and more established brand, which would go further in winning the riding back for the Conservatives.

I had a choice to make. I could turn my back and walk away, throwing my hands in the air and saying to hell with a system that I was becoming more disillusioned with by the day. Or I could take a deep breath, accept that I was going to bear the brunt of the public's response, and do my best to win this election anyway, on behalf of my friends and neighbours in my riding. And that's what I decided to do.

(I never got the former candidate's blessing publicly, by the way, but I did get it privately. That was important to me. The public perception didn't really matter, but I needed him to know that not only did I have nothing to do with this behind-the-scenes decision—I didn't even *know* about it until I arrived in Nova Scotia.)

So I went back to the EDA, and I was pretty straight-forward with them. I said, "Look, I clearly had no idea what I was walking into. It's obvious now that I was walking into a fire. Most people would tell you to shove it up your woohoo and go home, but I don't serve for my own purposes. What kind of example would I be setting for my children if I wasn't ready and willing to bear the brunt of this situation?"

In the end, most of the EDA supported me as the new candidate. There were still those who wanted to go through the full nomination process, probably because they had another choice who they liked better than me. But that was fine. I didn't bear them any grudge for having a different opinion.

But now we were in a difficult situation, because we were months behind in our campaign strategy. So we quickly put together a team, built around Rob Wolfe as my campaign manager. Rob is a wonderful man, very soft-spoken, and just so smart when it comes to politics. We had great people all the way down, from Ruth in the New Glasgow office, to Monica at Antigonish, to all the volunteers. I've done a lot of volunteering in my life, but the level of dedication from the people on my campaign was remarkable. I don't think I would have had the same energy and tenacity to do what they did, day in and day out.

I did plenty of door-knocking, of course, and most of the people I spoke to were fantastic. They thanked me for stepping up—even though some of them went on to say they couldn't support me because they didn't know who Andrew Scheer, then the leader of the Conservative Party of Canada, was. They would have been happy to support me individually, but they didn't trust the new leader of the party I was representing. Whereas they very much knew who Justin Trudeau was. I have to say, I loved that honesty. We live in a democracy, and everyone should feel proud and safe to speak their mind.

At other doors, however, I really witnessed what it means to have your character questioned. I was insulted. I was spit at. One old lady hit me with her cane. At first, I took that sort of thing personally. But eventually I realized these were people who were just frustrated with our entire political system. Their voices weren't being heard, and this was the only way they felt they could get anyone's attention.

There was one house that really showed me how readily some people will believe anything they're told. Somewhere along the campaign trail we'd caught wind of volunteers for another party telling people that I wasn't from Pictou County after all. They were saying I was born and raised in Alberta, and that anyone who said anything different was lying. It was petty nonsense, obviously, so at first I didn't think anything of it. But then I knocked on this one door, and an elderly gentleman answered it. Before I could say a word, he looked at me and said, "You get on your horse and get back to Alberta, where you're from." With a few choice expletives thrown in. Then he slammed the door in my face.

I took a step back. And then I just started laughing. Because I honestly didn't know how to deal with what had just happened. Obviously, this man was misinformed. But he should also probably be grateful that I'm as patient as I am. My only response was laughter, even though there was a part of me that had to bite my tongue and walk away from that door, rather than go through it.

I learned something in that moment—about the ignorance of others, but also about how different generations can be when it comes to trust in the media. When I was a kid, my mom and dad believed every single word that was printed in the newspaper or said on the evening news. A lot of older folks who I met while door-knocking were the same way, even when it came to things like social media. It kind of broke my heart. These days, you have to be a lot more careful about what you believe. Even in a situation like this, where I was the person who knew the truth better than anyone—it was *about me*, after all—people didn't want to hear about it if it conflicted with what they'd already heard.

I have lots of friends in the media, and I respect what they do, but the warning that the media needs to hear—from all Canadians—is: Please stay true to your job, which is printing the truth as best you can. Don't be distracted by those in power who have influence and money. Do the right thing. During my campaign, I witnessed the manipulation of a story firsthand with a writer and an outlet I won't name. This person's story was designed to hurt not just me, but also the party I was representing, and it disgusted me, because I knew there were going to be people out there who would believe it. The more I look at it, across the country and around the world, the more I see how this kind of misinformation helps create divisiveness. The media has an opportunity to bring it all back to the truth, which is all that counts in the end. I pray for those who are doing the right thing and have to put up with those who aren't.

I would still encourage anyone to step up and run for office if they feel the call. But before you do, make sure you vet everything you're being told. Don't do what I did and assume that everyone has your best interests at heart. Make sure that the people who are supposed to be working for you are actually doing that, and not just furthering their own interests. That's what still bugs me the most. So many people gave so much of themselves, only to get crapped on by the system.

On the evening of the election, I walked into our official campaign venue with no idea what was going to happen. What did the Lord have planned for me this time? I'd stepped up and done my best, but was that enough? When we eventually heard that my opponent, Sean Fraser, had been re-elected for the Liberals, I went over to his venue—which was just across the street—and officially conceded. We shook hands and agreed to meet up and talk a few days later, which we did.

Was I disappointed? Absolutely. I wanted the Conservative Party to win, because I've been a true-blue conservative my whole life, just like my parents were before me. But I didn't harp on that disappointment for too long.

Since that time, I've stayed closer to politics, talking more with guys like John Barlow and R. J. Sigurdson, who's our provincial member of the legislative assembly here in Alberta. I've had wonderful conversations about politics with all of them, and I know they're there for the right reasons.

In fact, I've been lucky in my life to have had many political mentors over the years. I first met Elmer MacKay, Peter's dad, when I was a little boy. My dad always treated Elmer with such reverence, and I learned a lot from him as well, both as a kid and then again during my campaign. We can learn so much from the way things were done back then, politically, compared to how they're being done today.

Then, of course, there's Elmer's son Peter, who I consider a brother. I witnessed firsthand the work he did with our troops, and my goodness, did the troops love him. Here was a man who wasn't in uniform, yet who was revered and given respect by the troops anyway. That spoke mountains to me about Peter's character. He isn't admired because he's a politician. He's admired because of the man he is, and I'm proud to call him a friend.

Finally, Tim Houston has been such an inspiration to me over the years. These days, of course, Tim is the premier of Nova Scotia, but I knew him well before that, and we still have long conversations about every topic you can imagine. He and his wife even volunteered on my campaign, which still humbles me. Talking to someone like Tim, another person who's in politics for the right reasons, is really encouraging to me after witnessing so much negativity.

I still have opinions on lots of things, of course. For instance, I believe that when you become a politician, you should only be able to serve one term. If the country were run that way, you would have more people involved, from all walks of life. In a democracy, everyone has a story, and everyone's opinion matters. Out here in the west, everyone knows that in a federal campaign, by the time the votes in Manitoba have been counted it's already over. That's really deflating. I think we need to develop a system in Canada where everyone has an equal voice—because everyone does.

In the end, I don't regret stepping up to run. Not one bit. Being able to serve my country was an incredible experience, and I learned a lot, even if it wasn't the outcome I would have chosen. When people ask me if I would ever consider running again, there's a big part of me that thinks, *Yeah, I'll run—run from it.* But I believe I will, even though I'm still a little gun-shy from what happened last time. I've had a servant's heart since I was little, and I'll die with one as well. So I really have no choice. I have to go with how He made me.

Next time, however, I'm going to make sure I have every piece of information available to me before I decide. That way, if I end up walking into the fire again, I can at least know it's my fault my feet are smoking.

## Chapter Fifteen

# MUSIC LESSONS

E very artist has what I call career songs. These are the songs that are part of your legacy, and which will ultimately outlive you. Johnny Cash, obviously, had a lot of career songs. But so did George Jones, Michael Jackson, Prince—the list goes on.

I've been blessed enough to have three of them.

"My Name" is one. "I Want You to Live" is another. And "Just Like You" is my third career song. I wrote it for my son, Kale, when he was ten years old, and it's about the special relationship between a father and his son.

The song originated when my manager at the time asked me if I was interested in writing with Chad Kroeger of Nickelback. Obviously I knew who Chad was—a country boy who sings rock music. Just before we were scheduled to meet up, Chad called me and said, "Hey, would you mind if Richard Marx joined us?" I just about fell off my chair. I'd been a huge fan of Richard's since I was young, and his songs had soundtracked all of the dances of my youth. When a Richard

Marx song came on, you always hoped you could find someone to dance with, pronto.

Richard and I got along really well together, and I tried
not to fanboy out too hard. But I couldn't resist asking him
to play me a bit of "Right Here Waiting" on his acoustic
guitar—he agreed, but only after I promised I'd look away
while he played, to minimize the awkwardness of singing this
incredibly romantic song to a guy he'd just met. We ended
up writing for two of my records together. This was one
more crazy dream come true. I never once thought I'd end
up meeting him, let alone writing music with him, let alone
having him produce me, let alone being able to one day call
him a friend.

Of all our sessions, though, "Just Like You" was the stand-
out. It was partly inspired by Kale always asking me why I'd
written a song about his sister, but never about him. When I
brought the premise to Richard, he responded right away, because he's the father of sons as well. So he knew exactly what
I was talking about. Of course, my love of that song isn't to
discredit any of my other songs, especially fan favourites like
"Drinkin' Thinkin'," which audiences request all the time. But
"Just Like You" was a special moment, and I'm so proud of
how it came out.

I've recorded a lot of songs in my career, and most of them
contain a piece of me. I can admit, however, that there are
others that don't have much to do with me at all. We recorded
them just to chase radio. What I mean by that is that radio
stations were looking for a certain type of song, and we tried
to give them what they wanted to stay in rotation. Without
radio as a partner, especially in the age before social media,
it was tough to get your name out there and let people know

you had new music out, or that you were touring. Radio has been very kind to me over the years, and I know some stations played me even when they might not have liked a particular song, just out of respect for who I was and what I stood for. I'm grateful for that.

There are so many people who touch our music industry here in Canada, and I'm not sure they know how much we appreciate them and all that they do. When your team wins the Stanley Cup, the captain gets to hoist it first. But all those other players, the coaches, the staff, the trainers—every one of them plays a vital role, too. It's no different in our industry. Before I go on the road, we have pre-tour meetings with all our crew members, and I always take the time to thank them and show that I appreciate their hard work.

One thing I always used to catch crap for was trying to help the crew load and unload trailers. Eventually the rest of my band gave up on me, and said, "Let him go. He needs to do this, for some reason." Once we were getting our gear packed back up after a show in Nova Scotia in the freezing rain and snow, and everyone was moving extra quick. My manager tried to get me to go inside, but I insisted on helping, and, sure enough, whacked myself on the trailer door and cut my head wide open. There was blood everywhere, and I ended up giving myself a slight concussion. But it didn't matter. Like my dad said, you can't ask someone to do something that you aren't willing to do yourself.

Funnily enough, that story followed me around for years afterwards. Whenever I would walk into a venue, the local guys would say, "Hey, don't go anywhere near *our* gear!" It's moments like that where you realize just how small and tight-knit our industry really is.

Over the course of my career, I've learned a lot of lessons about the music industry, and while I don't complain about anything that's happened to me personally, I do feel a responsibility to the next generation of artists who are coming up in the industry today.

It was hard for me, working hand to mouth on the road for all those years, or scraping together $75 each week while Jen worked three jobs to support us. When the opportunity for better and higher-paying gigs came along, I couldn't say no. I'd been subconsciously trained to work, work, work. But I wish there had been somebody there to say to me, "Take a breath. The gigs aren't going anywhere." I should have been there to take my son to the bus stop on his first day of elementary school instead of being away, playing a show in—wherever it was. I don't even remember now. But I do know I wasn't there for him in that moment. And that's something I'll never forget.

That's why I really try to encourage other artists, especially younger ones, to enjoy the time with their families as much as they possibly can. Of course, it's easier said than done, because everyone has to make hay while the sun shines—especially in our industry, where nobody really knows just how much sunshine they're going to get.

Another thing I really advocate when talking to newer artists is ignoring the pressure they face to move away. From the get-go, younger country artists across Canada are told that they have to live in Nashville if they want to have a career. I know that's what I was told. And, look, if that's what they truly want to do, then great. Nashville is an awesome city. But nobody should ever feel like they *have* to do that to survive, especially now that we have social media to help get our music out there.

The fact of it is, there's no reason Canada can't drive our own country music industry in a big way. We have so many talented artists. We have record labels. We have radio stations. We have places to play shows, and places to buy records. And we have 38 million Canadians eager to hear great music. Why not here?

I take pride in having mentored quite a few up-and-coming artists. The first time I saw Brett Kissel play, he was fourteen, opening for me at the Canadian Finals Rodeo, and Jen and I both commented on how talented this kid was and how far he was destined to go. What I love about Brett is that he's always made music for himself above all. It doesn't matter what genre it's in, it has to move him—and that's a piece of advice I give to artists of the next generation all the time. When an artist is playing something they truly love, you can feel it, even in a recording. You may not believe me, but it's true. When I get in the studio as an engineer with someone who has that kind of energy, I can feel it coming through the headphones.

If you ever want to test this theory for yourself, pull out your phone and record yourself saying something into it—but say it with a frown. Then do the same again, only this time smiling. When you listen back and compare the two recordings, you'll hear what I mean.

When COVID hit, in early 2020, it devastated the music business. For me, it made me realize that I'd been taking the luxury of playing music for a living for granted. The pandemic was a slap upside the head and a kick in the pants, all at the same time.

But, as with living with type 1 diabetes, you have to find the positives. And so I did.

One benefit, of course, was that our family got to spend more time together than we had in a long while. Our kids couldn't go anywhere, so we all hung out as a family, playing games at the table, watching movies, stuff we hadn't done since they were little. It was a wonderful time for Jen and me as parents, but I think it was good for Madi and Kale, too. They got to reconnect with us and realize that we weren't so bad after all—maybe that we were even kind of cool. Mom is, anyway. Dad does his best.

The pandemic also forced me to reconsider my relationship with music. Without the ability to play live shows, I realized that I'd been getting a bit stagnant in how I'd been doing things. So I started doing online concerts. Every Sunday I'd play for an hour, totally free, for all the people out there who were stuck at home like I was. And what a revelation they were. I mean, I knew I had a supportive fan base, but for a couple of those shows, we had more than 210,000 people watching all at once—more than you could ever fit inside a single concert venue.

When I heard about some kids who weren't able to have their birthday parties because of COVID, I decided that one of my Sunday shows would be a kids show, during which I would play the songs from a kids record that I wrote, but never released, back in the early 2010s when my own kids were young. My performance of a piece called "The Fart Song" even had a guest appearance by my son's French bulldog, whose farts are famous for being able to clear an entire room. Naturally, he farted during the show itself, too. This wasn't ideal from a performance point of view, since it smelled so bad that my eyes started to water. But it felt somehow appropriate.

Playing for people online can be an odd experience, because when you finish playing a song, there's no applause. It's just silence. But a few weeks after that kids concert, I got a totally unexpected bit of feedback: a phone call from the head of CBC Kids, asking me if I'd be interested in developing a TV show for children.

I'd never thought about it, but once I did, the idea really started to appeal. I loved making that children's record that was never released, and of course I'd worked with countless kids over the years, in different scenarios and for different causes. But a TV show was a whole new frontier. Would anyone watch Mister Rogers if he was a cowboy?

I decided to find out. We created *Happy Trails*, a show where I play a character called Cowboy George, and I live on a farm along with a bunch of talking puppet friends, including a horse named Tilly, a chicken named Chu Chu, a goat in a wheelchair, a bunch of worms, and lots more. There are live songs, and dancing, and stories with nice lessons at the end. The show is aimed at preschoolers, but I wouldn't be surprised if some older kids, and maybe even their parents, tune in as well when it airs.

I started playing those free live concerts over the internet for no reason other than it seemed like a fun way to pass the time, but I felt my love of music come back twice as strong. Those online concerts showed me a couple of things. One, that there were a *lot* of people out there with time on their hands. And two, that music really is a healer. I was recently teaching a class in songwriting, and I said to the students, "Next to the power of prayer is the power of music." I really believe that. Music is built into us from the day we're born. When a baby coos, they're singing. It's as natural as breathing air. I know it always makes me feel better to pick up a guitar and start playing, but I was reminded that listening to music can also help soothe the mind in difficult times. When you get right down to it, music isn't about hitting a string, or a piano key, or a drum. It's about giving a little piece of yourself to whoever's out there listening. I'm always happy to do my part.

## Chapter Sixteen

# MY COUNTRY

E verything happens for a reason. When I was first diagnosed as a type 1 diabetic, part of the lesson I needed
to learn was to slow down—because I no longer had a choice.
Over time, I learned that God had taken something in my life
that was bad and turned it into a positive. I've said it many
times, but if I never got that diagnosis, then I would never
have gotten to go to the places I've been, or meet the people
I've met, or do the many incredible things I've gotten to do.
As strange as it sounds, in a way I'm grateful for that diagnosis. It allowed God to take me where I needed to go, and to
help me mature in the ways He knew I needed to.

Though I'm not sure if I would call myself mature, even
now. I'm still a big kid at heart, and probably always will be.
But when I look back on my fifty-two years and counting on
this earth, thirty-two of which have been spent in the music
business, I'm more aware of time passing than I used to be.
Every time you take a step forward, you don't get to go back.

Jen always tells me to remember to enjoy the journey, but

that's something I've always struggled with. As a kid, my head was in the clouds, daydreaming about my future in the air force. Even now, I *want* to sit back and be in the moment, but too often my mind floats away, thinking about what the next tour will look like, or what the next album will sound like.

In some ways, having such a strong imagination has been helpful in my life and my career. It's what has allowed me to be a songwriter. It's also what lets me come up with ideas for music videos, stay involved in a variety of charity and volunteer work, and even do a bit of acting over the years.

I've been lucky enough to appear on a couple of episodes of *Trailer Park Boys* where I was cast as a forest ranger, alongside my buddy Dave Gunning. Dave's character on the show didn't originally have a name, but when we got to set, I blurted out that he should be called Amanda. The crew thought that was funny, and it stuck. So for all seven days of shooting, just outside of Halifax, Dave was referred to as Amanda—I even got to call him that on-screen.

I've also gotten to appear in a couple of Christmas movies, which I know some people find corny. But I've always loved them, so when the chance to be in one came along, I couldn't pass it up. And I suppose I'm a natural fit for cowboy movies as well. Although the weird thing is that in almost every cowboy movie I've appeared in, my character has been shot dead. I'm not sure why. The only one I survived was *Dawn Rider*, starring Christian Slater—except there I ended up getting sick in real life, because I had to smoke a cigar for six hours while filming a scene. I don't know if you've ever had to smoke cigars for six hours straight, but I can't say I would recommend it.

In the end, though, I'll always come back to music. I love

singing the classics that I cut my teeth on in bars, and without which there would be no George Canyon today.

And I love writing what I call "cowboy songs," because that's who I have always been at heart. When Jen and I are out there working the ranch, riding the land, and checking cattle, we are at such peace. We love every second of every day. Whenever I'm out on the land I think back to watching John Wayne movies with my papa, as a kid in Pictou County. He'd been a Nova Scotia cowboy, and he told me that if I wanted to, one day I could be a cowboy, too.

So if you ever need to find me, God willing, I'll be at the ranch. For the rest of my life, that's the plan: raising cattle, riding horses—and making music.

# ACKNOWLEDGMENTS

Firstly, I just want to say: thank you so much for reading this book. Did I ever think I would write a memoir? Nope! Not a chance. I was first asked fifteen years ago, not long after *Nashville Star* aired, but at the time I said no. I didn't feel I had enough to offer and wasn't even sure what I would talk about. Only now do I have enough life experience behind me to justify setting out on a project like this.

Now that the finish line is in sight, it means the world to me to have gotten to do this with the support and faith of a publisher as great as Simon & Schuster, including my editor, Sarah St. Pierre, and the rest of the team there. And getting to work with my ghostwriter—well, let's just say you should all be very grateful that I have someone like Michael Hingston on my side, taking my stories and turning them into literature. Without him, this book would read a lot more like *Curious George*.

If I were to sit down and name every person in my life, both past and present, who has helped me, supported me, listened to me, put up with my bull poop, given me advice, shared my life experiences, and so much more, I would fail drastically, for the list would outweigh the words on the pages of this memoir. I thank each and every one of you, and you know who you are, for your patience, your kindness, your love, and your support, not only for me, but for Jen and the kids as well.

My faith and relationship with my Lord and Saviour Jesus Christ have been first and foremost in my life since I was five years old. I believe in the faith of my God who has blessed me through the good times and the bad. I not only acknowledge His love and blessings throughout this memoir but also through every step I take in the life He has given me. I thank Him daily for each and every one of you who has taken the time to be there for me and mine.

God bless you all.